Project Resilience

Beyond prescriptive project literature, we need to understand real projects, with real people and wicked problems. This book provides a structured approach, looking at traps or 'lures' (certainty, aleatoric risk view, over-simplicity, fail-safe over-planning, illusion of control). The book recognises 'too difficult' aspects that are often ignored, and best practices – a good contribution to the new way of looking at real projects.

Terry Williams, Hull University Business School, UK

Insightful and down to earth – this book is compulsive reading for anyone with an interest in Project Management. As the authors say, the purpose of this book is 'to guide – not prescribe' and in so doing it takes the reader through the subject matter in both its science and art forms. In so doing it provides a bridge between theory and practice using as it does some interesting vignettes to develop its themes. The aim is to improve the understanding of the 'practice' of project management in all its forms and to provide useful, thought-provoking approaches to disentangle the myths of the subject matter. There are many practical tips for the practitioner set out by authors who clearly know and understand the subject matter. I believe this book makes a useful contribution to the current literature.

Mike Jones, Director of the Foundation for Management Education, UK

This very readable book addresses some very common causes of serious project problems and even failures – the interplay of uncertainty and complexity and accommodating the different perceptions of those involved. The authors' insights, plus the well exemplified and very practical approaches described, will enable project managers to avoid many of the resulting risks and enable effective responses if they occur.

John Ward, Cranfield University, School of Management, UK

This thoroughly researched book provides fresh insights and perspectives to help the most capable project managers manage risk and deliver change in an increasingly uncertain and volatile world. For those new to the role it provides wisdom that can take a career to obtain by focusing on the art of delivery, or leadership, rather than on the science.

Donnie MacNicol, Director of Team Animation, UK

In major projects it is often said that 'the hard things are easy and the soft things are hard'. Managing the risks associated with people is far harder than managing those associated with engineering or technology. This book helps to address these more difficult challenges which emerge in complex and uncertain situations using more than just risk registers and tick boxes.

Manon Bradley, Development Director, Major Projects Association

A real refreshing new look at project management, pulling together recent research on how to deal with some of the challenges now being faced by project managers in the ever more complex project environment. Whereas traditional project management techniques and disciplines are essential, a project manager needs so much more if they are to be successful and this book is indeed a great help.

Dave Gunner, The PPM Academy

Project Resilience

The Art of Noticing, Interpreting, Preparing, Containing and Recovering

ELMAR KUTSCH, PhD
Cranfield University, UK

MARK HALL, PhD
Birmingham Business School, UK

NEIL TURNER, PhD
Cranfield University, UK

GOWER

Published by
Gower Publishing Limited
Wey Court East
Union Road
Farnham
Surrey, GU9 7PT
England

Gower Publishing Company
110 Cherry Street
Suite 3-1
Burlington, VT 05401-3818
USA

www.gowerpublishing.com

British Library Cataloguing in Publication Data
A catalogue record for this book is available from the British Library

ISBN: 9781472423634 (hbk)
ISBN: 9781472423641 (ebk – ePDF)
ISBN: 9781472423658 (ebk – ePUB)

Library of Congress Cataloging-in-Publication Data
Kutsch, Elmar.
 Project resilience : the art of noticing, interpreting, preparing, containing and recovering / by Elmar Kutsch, Mark Hall and Neil Turner.
    pages cm
 Includes bibliographical references and index.
  ISBN 978-1-4724-2363-4 (hardback) -- ISBN 978-1-4724-2364-1 (ebook) -- ISBN 978-1-4724-2365-8 (epub) 1. Project management. 2. Risk management. I. Title.

 HD69.P75K875 2015
 658.4'04--dc23

2015015560

Reprinted 2015

Printed in the United Kingdom by Henry Ling Limited, at the Dorset Press, Dorchester, DT1 1HD

Contents

List of Figures

List of Tables

Preface

In recent decades, the function of project management has become significantly more professionalised and is recognised as a key contributor to organisational success in both the public and private sectors. It is the way that organisational strategy is executed, the way that change is brought about. Doing this well is a major contributor to economic growth worldwide, so progress in project management is to be applauded.

Numerous prescriptive project management guidelines have been developed with the underlying premise that by following a set of rules, procedures and techniques, project success becomes attainable, some may even say inevitable. These tools are certainly very valuable, yet numerous studies have indicated that project performance across a range of industries is still disappointing. We need more than 'process' to get better.

In this book we acknowledge that in real projects we often have far less foreknowledge of events than we would like. Mostly our plans are estimates – 'best-guesses' – and certainty is far from assured. Projects include risks we can determine and prepare for and uncertainties that may surprise us. In short, we live in a complex world that is often not amenable to clear-cut solutions.

Our aim here is to go going beyond compliance to rules and procedures. We greatly respect the 'science' of project management, but we also have to consider the 'art'. We need to incorporate human creative skill, experience, and imagination in dealing with uncertainty. We discuss how our cognitive limitations hinder us in our desire to manage adversity, but also provide ideas about practical steps managers can take to deal better with risk and uncertainty.

Our hope is that these ideas will assist you in managing project adversity more effectively, and in helping to prevent crises from happening. However, our view is that it is not about 'if' but 'when' trouble will strike, so preparation is key, together with an ability to recover the project afterwards. We take a 'mindfulness' approach to project management, including building on individual and organisational behavioural attributes that aid in the recognition of, adaptation to, and recovery from, adversity. It is a 'human' approach, recognising the artful requirements that project managers need to be both successful and satisfied with their projects and their careers.

Chapter 1
THE CHALLENGE

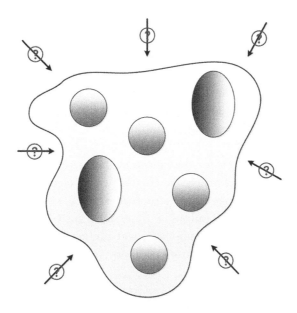

Many authors treat projects and project management with a strongly 'mechanistic' approach. The work can be broken down, executed and controlled as a series of interlocking parts. This is the technical, engineering-based conceptualisation, probably derived from the roots of the subject in large research and development projects. While acknowledging the many benefits of this view, we take a slightly different approach. We understand projects as 'organic' constructs, living entities existing for a finite period of time, consisting of people, structures and processes. They exist to deliver short term outputs and long terms outcomes for a parent organisation or a set of stakeholders. To continue the biological metaphor, this organism is constantly challenged by environmental adversity – risk, uncertainty and complexity. Success depends on remaining resilient, which we view as the ability to notice, interpret, prepare for, and consistently to contain and recover from such adversity.

This chapter is about those attacks on this entity we call a project. We will introduce you to ideas and mechanisms for resilience in project management and provide you with insights into how adversity in the form of risk, uncertainty and complexity can jeopardise project performance.

A Litany of Project Failure

In 2000, Airbus undertook the massively ambitious project of developing the A380 Superjumbo. In the spring of 2005, the production facilities in France and Germany began blaming each other publicly when deliveries were postponed from autumn 2005 to the spring of 2006. Then, in the autumn of 2006, the wiring harnesses from Hamburg failed to connect properly when the plane was assembled in the Toulouse plant. This made headlines across the world. Various reasons for the failure of the project were identified, from technical issues (different sites used different versions of the design software) to the unresponsive management structure, from a surprisingly balkanised organisational structure to a failure to understand customer needs adequately. This project was at least two years late, over budget in the order of €2 billion and incurred lost sales for the parent company in excess of €4.5 billion.

In the United States, the US Federal Bureau of Investigation (FBI) launched the Trilogy programme, a project to automate its case management. The project was initially conceived in three parts: the purchase of new desktop computers; developing secure, high-performance networks; and upgrading the FBI's suite of software applications. Although the first two parts were generally successful (although with major cost overruns) the last part proved a major headache, turning into a major project in its own right – the Virtual Case File (VCF). At the beginning of 2003, the FBI required an additional instalment of roughly $149 million. The accommodation of multiple change requests, scope creep and 'code bloat' led to the project finally being cancelled in 2005, still in the development stage and at a cost of $170 million.

The US government's Secure Border Initiative Network (SBInet) project was initiated in 2006 to utilise sensors and cameras along the 2,000 mile US border with Mexico. Boeing was appointed as the supplier on an indefinite delivery/ indefinite quantity contract. The instalment of this system ran into problems very quickly for a host of technological reasons, including its oversensitivity to rain and other non-alien related influences. After a series of technical glitches Homeland Security froze all funds allocated for an expansion of the fence. It was decided that SBInet could not meet its original objective of providing a single, integrated border security solution, but this was only after major expenditure.

These are just some examples of major projects that have run into trouble because of inadequate project management. A common theme running through these cases is that, despite having applied a plethora of deterministic project management practices, they still did not deliver as expected. This is not because their approach to compliance by 'designing' adversity out of the project was inadequate. It is rather that the situation-specific novelty in each case was perhaps too much for the past-informed rules and procedures and that the organisations' ways of working did not accommodate the reality of the situation. In a nutshell, they were not resilient enough.

This book looks at weaknesses with current thinking in project management and how projects can develop awareness, robustness and responsiveness to deal with risk, uncertainty and complexity. The aim is not so much to eradicate all these forms of adversity from project delivery – we think this is impossible. Rather, our objective is to help project managers find ways to notice more, interpret adversity more realistically, prepare themselves better for it, and contain and recover from it quicker and more appropriately. In short, the book is about making projects and project managers more resilient.

The Emergence of Project Management

We need to start with a common understanding of what is meant by the term 'project'. A project is commonly defined as a temporary endeavour with a specific beginning and end. It is characterised by the achievement of unique goals and objectives, and resources are limited. In contrast to business-as-usual activities, which are repetitive and permanent, projects often involve greater risk as well as uncertainty. At the outset of a project, managers may not know and understand exactly what they are required to achieve and how best to go about it, nor what changes and problems may be thrown at them. The discipline of project management has emerged in an attempt to aid managers facing these challenges.

A Brief History of Project Management

Mankind has achieved magnificent project outcomes for thousands of years. Marvels such as the Pyramids of Giza, the Great Wall of China, the Parthenon, and Stonehenge were constructed without modern-day techniques and software tools, although often with abundant yet expendable human resources. The twentieth century, though, experienced a new age of industrialisation and a drive towards repeatability of manufacturing outputs, mass-production and the pursuit of greater order and efficiency. Considered a milestone in the development of project management, Henry Gantt (1861–1919) developed the Gantt Chart. It illustrates the phases and tasks of a project schedule so that they can be understood easily.

The 1950s marked the emergence of the 'Program Evaluation and Review Technique' (PERT), deployed and exercised in the Polaris missile submarine programme. PERT displays how much time (involving the most likely, optimistic and pessimistic estimates) is allocated to a component of a project, such as a project task. It lays down interdependencies between these components that allow the definition of a critical path; any deviation or change from that path will have an automatic influence on the end date of the project.

Such techniques are now commonly applied in planning modern projects and often represent the core technique of management by planning. However, it was not until the 1960s that the development of these techniques led to the recognition of project management as a discipline. In 1969, the Project Management Institute (PMI) was founded. This not-for-profit project management organisation is one of the most recognised member associations in the world. It advocates providing project managers with a universal set of tools and techniques to manage projects successfully. As a consequence, the Project Management Body of Knowledge (PMBOK) Guide was published in 1987 [1]. Over the years, further internationally recognised frameworks and sourcebooks in project management have been developed, such as PRINCE2 and the Association for Project Management's (APM) Body of Knowledge. They form part of a wider narrative advocating a set of normative procedures that, if applied correctly, will lead to success.

Project Types

The construction of the first Pyramids, with new and marvellous artefacts as the outcomes, would today fall into the category of a New Product Development (NPD) project. NPD projects cover a multitude of types of work and may include the construction of a building, an IT system, or a new consumer product. A set of requirements is usually defined in advance and success is measured both by the project's achievement of 'producing' that item and its long term impact.

In Research and Development projects (R&D), the dominant focus is instead on a problem and the generation of new knowledge – a solution to the problem. If the emphasis is more on the 'R' than the 'D', then the outcomes can be less tangible than for NPD projects and may represent models or patents. That research stage may, though, lead to the 'D' phase and to the development of more tangible solutions.

These projects may not trigger any change in the providing party. 'Change' projects, however, are intended specifically to produce a desired change to a department, group, or entire organisation. Similar to NPD and R&D projects, at the outset change projects are defined by a problem, opportunity or a set of requirements.

For all these types of projects, regardless of whether they produce a tangible output, knowledge, or change, we want them to be successful. Newspapers are full of so-called 'failed' projects and many surveys have shown that the overall success rate of projects has remained stubbornly low for years. This begs the question: what exactly do we mean by success and failure when we talk about projects?

Project Success and Failure

Project success is a tricky concept. Projects are often assessed on the classic 'iron triangle' objectives of time, cost, and quality. Was it delivered on time, on budget, and did it meet the original performance specifications? If we rely on these three measures, then it may not be surprising if failure can be perceived as commonplace but there are problems with this for several reasons. Criteria drawn up in the early stages may turn out simply not to be correct. Knowledge-generation is inherent in many projects and initial expectations of accurate schedules and financial plans may be unrealistic. We need to be sensible with regard to what we expect to find out as part of the work and adjust expectations accordingly. Learning is often neglected as a key part of the project process. We do not argue with the importance of time, cost and quality, but they do represent a rather limited, short-term perspective of what constitutes success – and failure – in projects. Longer-term user or customer satisfaction after a project has been implemented, or the development of new organisational capabilities, are not necessarily captured by these measures. Projects that meet specifications, are on time and on budget may be a 'success', but if their outputs remain mostly unused because the end users were not adequately consulted, then the investment was a poor one. Spending a little more time and money mid-way through to deliver what is really necessary makes more sense, but if the organisational control and reward systems penalise this, they will drive the 'wrong' behaviours. Success and failure is thus far from clear-cut and 'simple' evaluations are often unwarranted.

We also have to realise that success and failure is a matter of perception. Perceptions matter, and they vary. Different stakeholders can have quite different views of how well the work went, and a single consensus view can be rare. A user who receives exactly the system he or she needs may not be overly worried about the budget over-run, but this may be the primary concern of the Finance Manager. So, whose success are we measuring?

Success perceptions will also change over time. For example, for all the woes that beset the Airbus A380 project, in the final analysis Airbus has a full order book and is quickly recouping the development costs through sales. Additionally, when compared with its only real competitor, Boeing, the development of the A380 was a success in comparison to Boeing's Dreamliner. Measures of project success need to go beyond the efficiency of the project work itself, also incorporating an evaluation of the long-term effectiveness of the endeavour.

We need, then, to ensure that we think more widely about the value of the projects that we undertake and take greater account of the intended purpose and benefits of the work, together with their actual impact. For example, the implementation of a new IT system may be intended to save costs in an organisation. For the owner or sponsor, this is the crucial aspect while the importance of meeting a project's quality, cost and time targets may actually be secondary. The bigger picture must be kept in mind.

In the light of this wider perspective on the nature of success, many projects that could be regarded as failures might actually end up being resounding successes (and, indeed, vice versa). Many projects, though, are still scrutinised on their efficiency targets, often with limited regard to whether the outcome produced is as useful as was intended. This myopic view of projects does not come as a surprise given that, for example, long-term satisfaction scores include soft factors that are difficult to establish and measure.

The Challenge of Risk and Uncertainty

A project's performance is constantly jeopardised by three components of environmental adversity: risk, uncertainty and complexity. Project managers are often explorers in the dark, trying to establish a planned state in an environment that tends to generate an adversity that is sometimes overt but sometimes only apparent when we stumble across it.

Risk and Uncertainty

Of course, potential adversity is not an unidentifiable 'thing'. For example, when throwing an unloaded die, it is possible to calculate exactly the probability of achieving certain results. This is what is known as aleatoric uncertainty, or true variability (from *alea* – the Latin word for die), and is how most people in organisations view risk – something that is identifiable and measurable. In most settings, it is the measurement of this kind of risk that is advocated, and this includes project management guidance. The occurrence of events in the past tells us how the future may unfold.

However, in many situations, we lack sufficient information to make a rational assessment of the probability of something happening. If our die were to constantly change its shape, it would be difficult or impossible to calculate the likelihood of outcomes actually happening. This is what we understand by the word uncertainty and it illustrates the distinction between uncertainty and risk – two words that are frequently conflated.[1] This particular type of uncertainty is known as epistemic uncertainty (from the Greek word for knowledge). In this case, our lack of knowledge about relevant variables leads to uncertainty. Hence, adversity in this book can be defined as follows in terms of:

- Risk: A calculable event that, if it occurs, may impact project outputs and outcomes
- Uncertainty: An incalculable event that, if it occurs, may impact project outputs and outcomes

Distinguishing between the two is important, although difficult. Risk is informed by the past. It is a future event, whose repeatable occurrence can be measured – quantified or qualified – with some confidence. In contrast,

---

1   A variety of definitions exist in the literature. Our aim is to provide a user-friendly definition of and distinction between risk and uncertainty by blatantly, although not unintentionally, disregarding most of the academic literature.

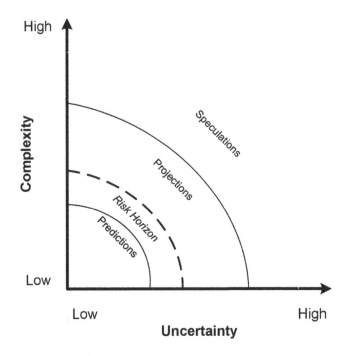

Figure 1.1   Risk horizon

uncertainty characterises a situation that is no more than an assumption, an immeasurable guess, which one struggles to attach numbers or to articulate. A risk is associated with clarity and predictability, uncertainty with novelty and ambiguity.

Time has a moderating effect on whether the future is risky or uncertain. In the short-term, our risk horizon is far more measurable and tangible (see Figure 1.1). The past allows us to make some judgement about the near future. The further out we move, the greater the amount of novelty and ambiguity. We face diminishing precision, and situations are more open to interpretation. The discipline of project management is challenging as we must peer into an uncertain future, often with the constraint of having stakeholders with fixed expectations.

Risk and uncertainty can be applied to key aspects of the project. There may be a lack of clarity with regards to the goal to be achieved and the best way to get there. These ideas may also change as the project unfolds.

Let us start with the first aspect of Goal risk/uncertainty. Imagine you start a project of a type you have not engaged in before. Neither you nor your stakeholders can fully define the goal of the project with reasonable confidence. This is not uncommon – many projects involve only vaguely definable outcomes that even key owners or sponsors struggle to specify. In R&D projects, for example, managers are faced with the challenge of specifying requirements, functions and outcomes, yet the reality is that knowledge will emerge as the work progresses.

The second dimension relates to the 'how' in the form of Approach risk/ uncertainty. Not only is the precise goal uncertain, but so too is the path towards it. Imagine you know what the goal is that needs to be achieved, but you do not know how to get there. Although 'ways of working' in projects are often advocated by professional organisations such as PMI as being universal, many projects have unique (and constraining) elements, such as the new technology involved or the relationships between the key participants. One size does not always fit all. The 'how' in the project can be a winding and uncertain path and, as such, managers may have to alter their initially-planned approach.

Environmental changes can necessitate adaptation. These can include stakeholders updating their requirements, the unforeseen acts of suppliers or competitors, changes in different parts of the organisation, and wider market turbulence. These are issues of Dynamic risk/uncertainty. Managing can be like standing on quicksand. Even when we know what needs to be achieved and how to achieve it, changes – sometimes outside our control – jeopardise both the goal and the way of achieving it, requiring a constant readjustment of our actions.

Finally, a category of risk/uncertainty that is often largely ignored by major project management frameworks is Relational. Risk/uncertainty is ultimately in the eye of the beholder. Despite the plethora of project data, people need to make sense of what they see. The same data can lead to multiple interpretations, and hence a variety of actions, which may be unhelpful. The sum of the responses to differing perceptions may add to the confusion. A shared understanding in the project team about what the data mean can lead to a more coherent, considered approach to dealing with the risks and uncertainties.

Reflection

How well do the following statements characterise your project? For each item, select one box only that best reflects your conclusion.

Goal Risk/Uncertainty	Not at all		To some extent		To a great extent
The outcome of the project is wide open.	1	2	3	4	5
We cannot quantify or qualify the goal with confidence.	1	2	3	4	5
There is nothing like this out there.	1	2	3	4	5

Approach Risk/Uncertainty	Not at all		To some extent		To a great extent
Our ways of working do not apply to this project.	1	2	3	4	5
We have never done something like it.	1	2	3	4	5
We need to take one step at a time.	1	2	3	4	5

Dynamic Risk/Uncertainty	Not at all		To some extent		To a great extent
Nothing remains the same here.	1	2	3	4	5
It is like standing on quicksand.	1	2	3	4	5
There are many changes going on at once.	1	2	3	4	5

Relational Risk/Uncertainty	Not at all		To some extent		To a great extent
No one is on the same page.	1	2	3	4	5
We all have a different understanding about where to go and how to do it.	1	2	3	4	5
Our goals are in conflict with each other.	1	2	3	4	5

Scoring: Add the numbers. If you score higher than 9 in each category, please define which aspects are uncertain. If you score 9 or lower in a category, it might be worth checking that your colleagues agree. A 'Not at all' answer may indicate that you are underestimating the extent of risk/uncertainty.

Complexity

The previous assessment unpacks the extent to which you perceive your project to be risky and uncertain. Be aware that not only risk and uncertainty may derail your project. There is also the third element of adversity, complexity.

- Complexity: Changing interrelatedness of risk and uncertainty.

Complexity characterises the interactions between risk and uncertainty, and the extent to and speed at which risk and uncertainty influence project performance. In a tightly coupled project, characterised by 'time dependent processes', 'little slack', 'invariant sequences of operations' [2–4], incidents can occur from initial (potentially small) failures building on themselves and rapidly becoming larger, triggering a sudden crisis (see Figure 1.2). To make matters worse, in striving for ever greater efficiency in projects, slack and buffers tend to get stripped out at the planning stage, activities in the Gantt chart are 'crashed', and projects become tightly coupled, removing any redundancy and thus 'space' to intervene.

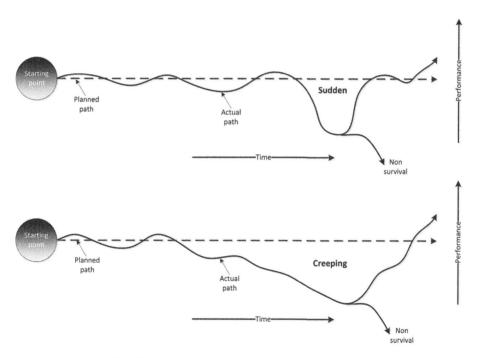

Figure 1.2   The differing dynamics of crises

In a loosely coupled project, on the other hand, risk and uncertainty have limited direct implications for the other components (e.g. tasks, resources) in a project. The project does not destabilise overnight and this allows a longer incubation phase – a creeping crisis – in which one has the opportunity to carry out some forms of intervention.

Reflection

How well do the following statements characterise your project? For each item, select one box only that best reflects your conclusion.

Complexity	Not at all		To some extent		To a great extent
There is a lot of redundancy (e.g. time buffers) in our project.	1	2	3	4	5
Not every task has to go right the first time.	1	2	3	4	5
We have time to correct failures.	1	2	3	4	5
What is happening is directly observable.	1	2	3	4	5
There are many different ways to manage this project. If something goes wrong, we can immediately switch to an alternative way of working.	1	2	3	4	5

Scoring: Add the numbers. If you score higher than 15, your project is relatively loosely coupled, with a lower chance of small failures rapidly triggering a crisis. If you score 15 or lower, please think whether the project needs to be 'decoupled', that is to say, whether complexity needs to be reduced to allow for timely interventions.

A tightly coupled project is more prone to a sudden destabilisation. If something fails or does not go as planned, it can create an immediate knock-on effect and small failures may quickly cascade into a full-blown crisis.

However, most projects do not face such a sudden collapse; they generally face a creeping erosion of performance, a 'death by a thousand cuts', a crisis that gradually builds. Most projects have a prolonged incubation phase, where risk and uncertainty gradually build to a crisis. Because of loose coupling, there is no speedy collapse of performance and it is possible that management actions can be purposefully executed in a timely manner, to prevent a crisis in the first place.

In many projects, great effort is spent transforming uncertainty into risk, with the aim of planning it out of a project. Usually, such effort to address project adversity, in advance of it happening, is satisfied through the key discipline of risk management.

The Evolution of Risk Management

The evolution of risk management – like many other planning mechanisms in project management – is characterised by the desire for certainty, quantification and the ability to prepare in advance for future events. In the distant past, people were guided by fate and a faith in God's will. Indeed, the future was perceived to be at the mercy of the gods. These long-held fundamental beliefs started to be challenged during the Renaissance, a period of turmoil, in which the shackles of superstition were challenged and inquisitive people such as Pascal and Fermat embraced the concept of forecasting and of building the foundations for the theory of probability.

Probability theory evolved quickly into a method of organising, leading to, for example, the mathematical basis for the insurance industry. Until the early twentieth century, human imagination was driven by repeatability and statistical analysis of the past to inform the future, and many of our modern approaches are based on probabilistic forecasting and decision-making driven by a concept called Expected Utility Theory (EUT). EUT states that decisions about risks are made by comparing their expected utility values, for example, the weighted sum of probability multiplied by impact, so that the utility of decision-making choices is weighted according to their probabilities and outcomes [5]. Consider the following simplified example shown in Figure 1.3.

In the diagram, the probability of avoiding risks in a project through the execution of a risk response action is P and without risk actions, Q, with P larger than Q and $1 - Q$ larger than $1 - P$. The utility of avoiding risks (relative to the cost of materialised risk) is A, and the utility of no actions (relative to the cost of those actions) is G while A is assumed to be greater than G. The decision by the project manager to take actions or not depends on the utility of avoiding the materialisation of uncertainty (benefit) while committing resources (cost), and on the relative magnitude of the objective or subjective probabilities.

EUT is a basic model of rational choice that underpins most methodologies for taking risky decisions [5] and is generally regarded as a very useful and effective framework for decision-making under risk [6]. However, the often 'blind' adherence to the principles of EUT and the resulting illusion of certainty

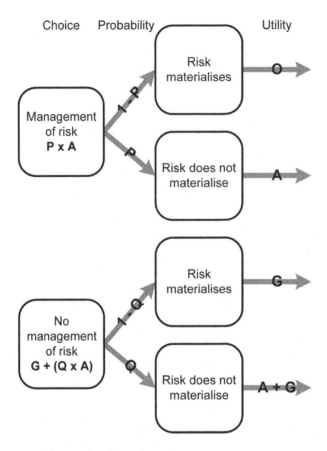

Figure 1.3   Expected utility theory

Note: The expected utility of taking risk response actions is $((1 - P) \times 0) + (P \times A) = P \times A$. The expected utility of not taking risk response actions is $((1 - Q) \times G) + (Q \times (A + G)) = G + (Q \times A)$.

was shattered by two bloody World Wars and, in more recent times, by major disasters such as the collapse of Lehman Brothers and the world recession, and the rise of world terrorism. Emerging criticism up to the present day has challenged the commonly adopted and advocated view that the past, if repeated often enough, can confidently inform the future [7]:

> *Those who live by the numbers may find that the mathematically inspired techniques of modernism have sown the seeds of a destructive technology in which computers have become mere replacements for the snake dancers, the bloodlettings, the genuflections, and the visits to the oracles and witches that characterized risk management and decision making in days of yore. [8, p. 51]*

WHAT THE LITERATURE SAYS ABOUT ...
Project Management as a Theory

Project Management as a 'stand-alone' discipline started to gain traction in the 1950s, in the heyday of Gantt's work. Already at that time, objections from academics and practitioners alike concerned the obsession with planning tools and techniques, of which risk management was one. Project management as an academic discipline has struggled to distinguish itself theoretically from other disciplines, such as Human Resource Management or Leadership. It has always been a subject of contention that project management is a subject that borrows from other disciplines and thus does not justify its own existence, as it is perceived as more of a practitioner discipline, not worthy of academic recognition.

Nevertheless, project management has started to carve out its own field and theory. One such theoretical 'lens' is the Theory of Temporary Organisations [e.g. 9,10]. This discrete body of literature is still new in comparison to other theories, or in other words, in comparison to other accumulated bodies of knowledge. In the 1990s a single paper summarised the apparent struggle of project management. Packendorff [11] criticised the fact that:

- there was an abundance of normative advice on what one should do but mostly with a lack of empirical evidence;
- projects were seen as a set of rules, procedures, tools and techniques and not as an impermanent organisational entity;
- and the professional bodies in project management make project management appear to be general theory that can be applied irrespective of the environment within which projects are exercised.

Such criticism has gone hand-in-hand with the ever increasing influence of professional standards which seem to drive the research agenda, rather than vice versa.

Standards in project management are various. Most dominant are those of the Project Management Institute (PMI), the UK Government Centre for Information Systems and the British Standards Institution, all of which offer similar, if not identical, standards for project management. Those offered by the PMI are widely used and are considered to be a competency standard [12]. The PMI standard *A Guide to the Project Management Body of Knowledge* (PMBOK) [13] covers multiple areas of project management knowledge.

The purpose of project management is seen as the management of entities such as tasks, requirements and objectives in advance, and is reliant on hindsight as a predictor for future changes. However, the problem that project management faces relates to the degree of uncertainty that is inherited by a project.

This problem, arising through the lack of hindsight, means that project managers cannot rely on the validity of probabilistic estimates about future risk based upon historical data [12, 14].

The PMBOK guide approach to 'best' practice project management standards, as introduced and promoted by organisations such as PMI or APM, appears to be self-evidently correct. In this respect, Williams [15, p. 498] argues:

> Project management as set out by the societies is presented as a set of normative procedures which appear to be self-evidently correct: following these procedures, it is implied, will produce effectively managed projects; and project failure is indicative of inadequate attention to the proper project management procedures.

That highlights again the uneasy coexistence between professional bodies of knowledge and the validation, but also criticism, from their research counterparts. In essence, the fundamental assumption of traditional project management standards is that the project is decoupled from its environment. That is to say, once the project is planned, changes should happen only occasionally. Assumptions of project management include rationality, knowledge of probable future states and repeatability of events [12], all under the umbrella of the Theory of Probability. But, to what extent can project managers rely on the validity of probabilistic conclusions about the future based upon historical data [12, 14]? In this respect Shakle [16, p. 5] argues:

> The theory of probability, in the form which has been given to it by mathematicians and actuaries, is adapted to discovering the tendencies of a given system under indefinitely repeated trials or experiments. In any set of such trials, each trial is, for the purpose of discovering such a tendency, given equal weight with all the others. No individual trial is considered to have any importance in itself for its own sake, and any tendency which may be inductively discovered or predicted a priori for the system, tells us nothing about any single individual trial which we may propose to make the future.

Frosdick [14, p. 176] adds: 'In the absence of adequate data, the assignment of probabilities is a subjective process dependent on the assigner's own bias.'

As a result, although project management in its prescribed form is a rational, normative set of processes, it faces the challenge of uncertainty influencing the project outcome [17]. The recognition of uncertainty by scholars and practitioners has led to new approaches in project management – exemplified by 'agile' project management [18]. Whereas 'traditional' project management focuses on a plan-design-build lifecycle, agile project management emphasises an organic, evolutionary envision-explore-adapt lifecycle [19]. For example, in software development, prominent 'agile' approaches of this type are Scrum, Dynamic Systems Development Method (DSDM), Crystal methods, Feature-Driven Development (FDD), Lean Development (LD), Extreme Programming (XP) and Adaptive Software Development (ASD) [20]. In contrast to traditional methodologies that emphasise 'management as planning', agile project management emphasises 'management by organising' [21], offering a higher degree of flexibility; for a project to be successful in an inherently uncertain environment, flexibility is assumed to be of major importance. As a result of the criticism facing traditional methods, Scrum is one of several agile methods used for developing and monitoring an IT project. It borrows some techniques from XP and other agile methods and theories. Scrum assumes that a problem cannot be fully understood or defined and that a project team should perform like a sports team working together to achieve a common goal. For example, the project development process is treated as a controlled black box instead of a fully defined and transparent process. Scrum concentrates more on maximising the team's ability to respond in an agile, flexible manner to emerging challenges [22]. It fosters a self-organising team environment by encouraging verbal communications across all team members and across all disciplines that are involved in the project. Scrum emphasises frequent meetings (iterative feedback) with both customers and stakeholders to ensure that a project's progress remains 'on track'.

Scrum and other agile approaches to managing a project have in common the fact that tasks are not planned in advance in the way that traditional project management literature recommends. Only prerequisites such as the allocation of resources for tasks are planned and these are revised on a daily or weekly basis. Changes are allowed late in the development cycle [20, 22].

Where does all this leave the discipline of project management? Project management has developed into a practitioner-driven discipline, powered by those hotly-contested normative, rule-based bodies of knowledge. Compliance with them seems paramount. Although the consistent application of these bodies of knowledge has provided substantial benefits and has undoubtedly increased the success rates of projects in recent times, they are not without limitations and even detrimental effects. Into this breach steps 'agile' project management, which seems to break free from (the illusion of) determinism and control. Once defined as a set of principles [19], agile ways of working are increasingly 'proceduralised', with an emphasis on compliance and non-situated human cognition.

One can only hope that empirical research sheds more light on what works and what does not, irrespective of whether project management develops its own theory as a distinguishing factor. There is a valuable opportunity to challenge the power of normative thinking and management, as advocated by project management associations. If more research brings to light the fact that failure in project management is not only associated with ' ... *inadequate attention to the project management procedures*' [23, p. 2], this may trigger a rethink of the prevailing project management discourse [24].

What this Book is About

This book has two purposes. It offers a glimpse into our tendencies to be irrational in the face of adversity – risk, uncertainty and complexity. Furthermore, it endeavours to challenge the often held view that quantification of the future and the 'automation' of actions can be an appropriate substitute for flawed human cognition. In short, although we respect the bodies of knowledge and the valuable work than has gone into the professionalisation of project management over recent decades, this represents the 'necessary but not sufficient' state of current knowledge. We need more.

The second purpose is to offer a new perspective to assist in managing risky and, in particular, uncertain and complex projects. We will provide insights into the project capability of resilience. This requires participants to notice risk and uncertainty more successfully, to be able to interpret situations more effectively, to prepare themselves and their projects adequately for uncertain situations and, importantly, to recover swiftly from issues after they occur.

This book goes beyond commonly-accepted standards in project management with the aim of providing an understanding of how to implement project-wide resilience. It identifies the principles associated with the management of risk, uncertainty and complexity – with an emphasis on the last two – from a predominantly behavioural perspective and offers a fresh outlook on how to be resilient in a real and practical sense.

But beware! It is not a book that should be used as a manual or set of standard operating procedures. It is not comprehensive, nor do we claim to have discovered the 'Holy Grail' of project management. The book's purpose is to guide, not to prescribe. It is best used as a trigger for a thinking process to define your own unique approach to managing uncertainty, not to replace your own experience and judgement. You should never outsource your thinking to a book. Ultimately, it has been written to challenge traditional wisdom in project management and to address the rationale for 'creative' best practices.

This book consists of eight chapters, each based on a separate stage of managing risk, uncertainty and complexity. This chapter sets the scene on adversity. Chapter 2 aims to distinguish between two archetypes of project management by exploring one of the most puzzling defeats in modern military history. Chapter 3 is about the art of noticing, how to anticipate the immeasurable and the unpredictable. In Chapter 4, we look at the question of how to make sense of adversity and how to judge it. A nuanced appreciation of a risky, uncertain and complex environment is followed by guidance for project preparation and readiness for it in Chapter 5. Containing adversity, responding appropriately, and receiving support in doing so is at the forefront of Chapter 6. Chapter 7 acknowledges that not all adversity can be designed out of a project. It is not a question of 'if' but of 'when' a crisis strikes and how we can recover from it. Chapter 8 brings it all together and there we reflect on how to activate and maintain a permanent state of project resilience.

Chapters 3–7 proceed in a specific format. Each has four main sections, tackling the 'lures' that make it difficult for a project to be resilient, what organisations can do to counter this, the role of leadership in driving resilient approaches and, finally, the way relationships across projects teams can be managed to ensure resilience is embedded.

A Section on Lures

The human brain is an amazing and incredibly powerful machine of synapses and neurons. But the brain is also fallible. It is not a super-computer, but has evolved as a social machine. The information it receives is partial and localised (what we sometimes call culture). As a result, our behaviour is subject to cognitive biases, those annoying glitches in our thinking that cause us to make questionable decisions and reach erroneous conclusions. We are emotional and partial beings – we are human. It is important to distinguish between cognitive biases and logical fallacies. A logical fallacy is an error in logical argumentation (e.g. ad hominem attacks, slippery slopes, circular arguments, appeal to force, etc.). A cognitive bias, on the other hand, is a genuine deficiency or limitation in our thinking – a flaw in judgement that arises from errors of memory, social attribution, and miscalculations (such as statistical errors or a false sense of probability).

As a result, we frequently behave irrationally in the way we deal with risk and uncertainty, in the way we perceive it, in the way we understand it and in the way we respond to it. We will start each chapter with some of these behavioural 'shortcomings'. People can walk, to some extent, 'brainlessly' through projects, driven by the original plan and what they are told to do. All we are doing in this section of each chapter is to point out some of the behaviours, learnt and emotional, that make the management of adversity difficult. All we ask is that project managers understand that these fallibilities exist; we hope they see our suggestions as ways of helping to overcome fallible human cognition.

A Section on Enablers

In order to deal with our fallibilities, we would like to suggest examples of 'good practice' – what a project manager could do (with an emphasis on 'could'). We want to emphasise that anything we suggest could be done to manage uncertainty is context-specific. What works in one context may not work in another. These are not hard-and-fast rules. In addition, we neither claim that the suggested practices to manage adversity comprise a complete set of actions, nor that they are invariably the practices that make a project more resilient. Rather, they are prompts to think differently about ways to acquire resilience. Please use this book to think about how our suggestions might apply to your own circumstances. Ask yourself why you might apply some and not others. Elaborate on the pros and cons. Do not fall prey to the temptation to take on a practice without tailoring it to your projects and, worse, without the support and buy-in of senior leaders and stakeholders.

A Section on Leadership

Having suggested the 'What' (although intentionally non-prescriptively), we follow with the 'How' of implementation. If one leadership style has seemingly conquered the project management world, it is that of transactional leadership. Transactional leadership relies very much on compliance with process and procedures, in which, as much as possible, situated human cognition is eliminated as a source of error through the imposition of rule-based behaviour. This approach does work if the project risks are predictable, measurable and controllable and people working on the project behave in reliable, rational ways. Unfortunately, management is rarely this straightforward. Resilient project managers, though, do not lead by replacing 'thinking'; they facilitate flexibility in mind-sets and empower people to learn and apply situational judgement. They encourage information flow and provide a culture of support and encouragement.

A Section on Relationships

Projects are social entities, often with a multitude of internal and external stakeholders. Whereas stakeholders add complexity, they can also be used as resources to manage risk, uncertainty and complexity more effectively. Managing adversity can be a journey of painful failure, sometimes on an enormous scale. Embracing it in a resilient manner means managing, and educating, stakeholders. Reluctance to give in to temptation and consider the future as certain is only the beginning of stakeholder management. Not least, it is an emotional rollercoaster that requires some dedicated preparation and intervention.

All the chapters in this book are complemented by two types of vignettes – indicated by text boxes – of best practices and evocative syntheses of key literature.

Best Practices

We try to learn from the best, and try to understand what they do and why. We have selected three organisations which we believe have a track record of successful project delivery (with only the occasional hiccup). They all carry out project work in a world of risk, uncertainty and complexity, yet they prevail. These project-based organisations rely on the principle of being compliant with rules and procedures, and rightly so. Yet, they do not stop there; they create a state of awareness beyond the past and ready themselves for the unpredictable future. When a crisis cannot be averted, response enactment is swift and pragmatic. Divergence from the expected plan does not result in simply tightening the book of rules and procedures, but includes questioning project resilience in the widest sense possible. The case companies are introduced in the following section and throughout this book, in which we draw extensively on interviews and conversations with key employees in each company. Later vignettes provide insight into 'How' they do it.

BEST PRACTICE

Our Case Companies

The Technology Partnership Group (TTP Group) is a technology and product development company formed in 1987. They operate in a number of diverse technology areas including industrial and consumer products, micro devices, medical and life sciences technology, and electronics. Their core offering is the rapid development of challenging new technology, which is enabled through their depth of scientific, engineering and business capability. TTP is one of Europe's leading independent product development companies, serving clients worldwide. The founding group of 30 investor employees had all worked for PA Technology, part of the PA Consulting Group. TTP remains majority employee owned. They are located close to Cambridge, with around 300 staff. Their turnover in 2013 was £39m.

TTP is an operating company within the TTP Group. Other companies in the group include TTP Venture Managers, which manages an early stage technology investment fund, TTP Labtech, which supplies instrumentation and custom automation to the Life Sciences sector, and Tonejet, which operates in the commercial and industrial printing markets. TTP Group also owns Melbourn Science Park, Cambridge UK, where TTP is based.

TTP operates in a highly uncertain business environment. Their core business is the creation of new technology, so there is always a degree of uncertainty in each of the 70–80 projects they might be working on at any given time. TTP have been involved in developing numerous technologies which then find applications in all sorts of areas. For example, TTP develops medical technologies such as the Bio-Seeq™ nucleic acid detection device. Elsewhere, they have developed propriety disc pump technology which has gone on to be used in a variety of medical devices. An example of a project that cut across organisational boundaries was the Sterishot, an obstetric surgical tool which combined engineering capabilities with human factor analysis to devise an ergonomic device to do the job. Another area in which TTP has undertaken development projects is communications technology. Examples include the development of terrestrial and satellite digital technologies for devices like the Roberts solar powered DAB radio and the development of the hardware for Vodafone's packet radio broadcast services. In electronics and sensor technologies, TTP helped Promethean develop the sensor devices for their latest generation of whiteboards. These are just some of examples of the many projects TTP undertakes in a wide number of technological development areas. Many of the technologies which TTP devises go on to be incorporated into products for mass or batch production and may be incorporated into devices which are used every day by companies and consumers.

The Aviva Group has a history stretching back more than three centuries. Over the years, many companies in a number of countries have been part of their rich history, including Norwich Union, General Accident, Delta Lloyd and Hibernian. In 2000, the Group changed its name to Aviva, a palindrome chosen for its worldwide appeal and ease of pronunciation in many tongues.

With a history traceable back to 1696, the group prides itself on being the oldest mutual life insurer. Being one of the oldest fire insurers as well as the first and only insurance company to hold royal warrants are amongst its notable achievements.

Currently Aviva provides 31 million customers with insurance, savings and investment products. It uses project management skills and techniques to deliver major changes and specific project objectives to support its overall plans. The types of change typically handled as 'projects' are customer service enhancements, digital innovation and legal and regulatory changes. An example of each type is given below.

Customer Service Enhancement

In 2014, as part of its commitment to improve its customer service, Aviva became the first UK Insurer to publish its customer claim reviews online to give new customers more information about the service they can expect to receive and, also, to provide an open and public forum for customers to feed back about their claims experiences.

The service works by sending an email to customers after they have had a claim settled, asking them to write a review and give a rating for the service they have received. Customers can give a rating out of five and write a short review which may then be posted on the website, commenting on the service, how the claim has been processed and the overall experience. Both positive and critical reviews are posted online to give customers an overall view of the service as well as the overall rating.

Digital Innovation

In 2014, Aviva launched its MyAviva app. This app lets customers access all their Aviva policies in one place, as well as offering a range of discounts and competitions via a secure environment that is compatible with all current mobile devices.

Using the MyAviva app, customers can perform a range of actions, wherever they are, which include the facility to:

- check the value of their pension or bond;
- access Aviva Advantages, Aviva's exclusive selection of special offers and rewards;
- access the new Aviva Life cover estimator tool, helping customers understand how much life cover could cost;
- renew car and home insurance, and set up renewal reminders;
- easily exchange policy details after a car accident;
- access loyalty discounts on a range of Aviva products;
- access helpful tips and information;
- be made aware of Legal and Regulatory changes.

Regulatory Changes

Aviva makes sure it keeps up to date with legal and regulatory changes in order to ensure that its customers are fully protected and informed. Recent examples of this include implementing the necessary changes in regulation brought about by the dissolution of the Financial Services Authority, and the creation of the Financial Conduct Authority, and ensuring compliance with the new pension laws.

Intel Corporation is an American organisation specialising in chip development and manufacturing. Back in 1968, two scientists, Robert Noyce and Gordon Moore, founded Intel® – the portmanteau abbreviation for INTegrated ELectronics – with a vision to produce semiconductor memory products. By 1971, they had introduced the world's first microprocessor. Most widely-known for processors, Intel is involved in the research and development of a variety of products and services related to communications and information systems. Its headquarters are located in Santa Clara, and by 2013 the company had over 107,000 employees worldwide.

An example of an activity Intel is engaged with is a high-value-adding project, destined to provide predictive analytics to Intel's sales organisation. This is to help the Intel sales force – Intel works with over 140,000 resellers who specify, design, build, and resell Intel-based technology products and solutions – optimise its account management and increase estimated incremental revenue.

At the beginning, Intel sold components to distribution, distribution sold to resellers and then resellers built the final product to be sold to end users. The market trend toward smaller mobile devices has changed channel dynamics. Larger original design manufacturers (ODMs) and original equipment manufacturers (OEMs) are now building the end product, such as a laptop, business Ultrabook™ device, or tablet, and then selling that product to distributors, who in turn sell it to resellers. The sales organisation tracks Intel components that are sold to the ODMs and OEMs, but little data are available after that. The result is that the sales organisation does not have the data it needs to support the reseller; specifically, what exactly the reseller is marketing that includes Intel technology. With a diverse customer base, the sales organisation needed assistance prioritising which customers should receive the most support, determining the optimal time in the customer's buying cycle to contact them, and deciding what products or support to offer.

Intel IT has developed an advanced predictive analytics solution to identify and prioritise which resellers have the greatest potential for high-volume sales. The enterprise-level, end-to-end predictive analytics engine is directly responsible for a portion of the sales organisation's increase in estimated incremental revenue.

The second type of vignette is a literature review, in which we summarise scholarly material on specific aspects. These vignettes are indicated by ...

What the Literature Says About

There is an incredible amount of written work out there, literature covering theoretical and empirical studies on managing risk, uncertainty and complexity, from which we have drawn our inspirations. These vignettes synthesise the key take-aways from each discrete body of literature. Usually, such literature reviews fill entire academic papers. We try to provide a short overview of the current state of the literature.[2]

With this book we hope to help you on a journey to increase and maintain your project resilience, by elaborating the 'What', the 'How' and the 'Why'. We offer a set of principles and a platform to reflect on your own context and your own projects, with self-assessment questionnaires throughout each chapter. It is ultimately **YOU**, as a project manager, or someone else involved in projects, who decides what is best applied to managing adversity in the form of risk, uncertainty and complexity – both efficiently and effectively.

References

1.   Project Management Institute, *A Guide to the Project Management Body of Knowledge*. 5th edition. 2013, Project Management Institute: Newtown Square, PA.
2.   Roberts, K.H., Managing High Reliability Organizations. *California Management Review*, 1990. 32(4): p. 101–13.
3.   Roberts, K.H., Some Characteristics of One Type of High Reliability Organization. *Organization Science*, 1990. 1(2): p. 160–76.
4.   Perrow, C., *Normal Accidents*. 1984, New York: Basic Books.
5.   Kahneman, D. and A. Tversky, Prospect Theory: An Analysis of Decision Under Risk. *Econometrica*, 1979. 47(2): p. 263–91.
6.   Einhorn, H.J. and R.M. Hogarth, Decision-making Under Ambiguity. *Journal of Business*, 1986. 59(4): p. 225–50.
7.   Bernstein, P.L., *Against the Gods*. 1998, New York: John Wiley & Sons.

---

2   In these literatures reviews, we have aimed to cover the key messages of specific bodies of knowledge. We have targeted some key sources, but we acknowledge that we have ignored many others.

8. Bernstein, P.L., The New Religion of Risk Management. *Harvard Business Review,* 1996. March–April: p. 47–51.

9. Lundin, R.A. and A. Soederholm, A Theory of the Temporary Organisation. *Scandinavian Journal of Management,* 1995. 11(4): p. 437–55.

10. Lundin, R.A. and R.S. Steinthorsson, Studying Organizations as Temporary. *Scandinavian Journal of Management,* 2003. 19: p. 233–50.

11. Packendorff, J., Inquiring into the Temporary Organisation: New Directions for Project Management Research. *International Journal of Project Management,* 1995. 11(4): p. 319–33.

12. Pender, S., Managing Incomplete Knowledge: Why Risk Management is Not Sufficient. *International Journal of Project Management,* 2001. 19: p. 79–87.

13. Project Management Institute, *A Guide to the Project Management Body of Knowledge.* 3rd edition. 2004, Pennsylvania: Project Management Institute.

14. Frosdick, S., The Techniques of Risk Analysis are Insufficient in Themselves. *Disaster Prevention and Management,* 1997. 6(3): p. 165–77.

15. Williams, T.M., Assessing and Moving on from the Dominant Project Management Discourse in the Light of Project Overruns. *IEEE Transactions on Engineering Management,* 2005. 52(4): p. 497–508.

16. Shakle, G., *Expectation in Economics.* 1952, Cambridge: Cambridge University Press.

17. Kutsch, E. and M. Hall, Intervening Conditions on the Management of Project Risk: Dealing with Uncertainty in Information Technology Projects. *International Journal of Project Management,* 2005. 23: p. 591–99.

18. Williams, T., The Need for New Paradigms for Complex Projects. *International Journal of Project Management,* 1999. 17(5): p. 269–73.

19. Highsmith, J., *Agile Project Management: Creating Innovative Products.* 2004, London: Addison-Wesley.

20. Highsmith, J., *Agile Software Development Ecosystems.* 2002, Boston: Addison-Wesley.

21. Williams, T.M., Assessing and Moving on from the Dominant Project Management Discourse in the Light of Project Overruns. *IEEE Transactions on Engineering Management,* 2005. 52(4): p. 497–508.

22. Schwaber, K., *Agile Project Management with Scrum.* 2004, Washington: Microsoft Press.

23. Williams, T., *Assessing and Building on the Underlying Theory of Project Management in the Light of Badly Over-Run Projects.* Proceedings PMI Research Conference, 2004.

24. Cicmil, S., et al., Rethinking Project Management: Researching the Actuality of Projects. *International Journal of Project Management,* 2006. 24(8): p. 675–86.

Chapter 2

ARCHETYPES OF PROJECT RESILIENCE

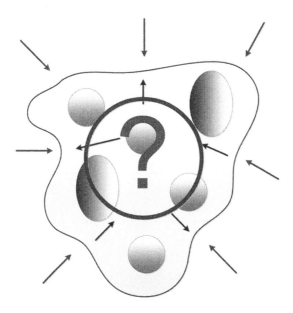

In the previous chapter we introduced the idea of projects as organic, 'living' entities. The resilience of a project 'organism' is aided by its being aware of its surroundings and potential disturbances in the forms of risk, uncertainty and complexity. It resists, absorbs and adapts to these disturbances without collapsing. In this chapter we continue on the roads to resilience by introducing and evaluating archetypes of project resilience which are often applied in an uneasy combination. One is based on rules and procedures, stripping the organism of situated thinking and relying wholly on predetermined responses to risk. The other allows human situated cognition – 'mindfulness' – to flourish, to counter the impact of uncertainty. We use a case study in which these two fundamentally different styles of management 'clashed' with each other – The Fall of France in 1940. In it, we try to analyse how risk and uncertainty were managed by the opposing parties, and what led to one of the most puzzling defeats in modern military history.

Acknowledging Uncertainty

In today's world, we face anything but 'perfect' knowledge. Adversity is normal and to be expected, and denying or ignoring its existence is generally foolish. Successful project managers accept these limitations on their ability to predict and control the future. What this means is that project managers acknowledge that the world is very much unpredictable, but not unmanageable.

Reflection

How well do the following statements characterise your project? For each item, select one box only that best reflects your conclusion.

Acceptance of risk and uncertainty	Not at all		To some extent		To a great extent
The planning of our project emphasises what we do not know, not only what we know.	1	2	3	4	5
We do not 'sell' this project, internally or externally as being guaranteed.	1	2	3	4	5
We are reluctant to underestimate risk and uncertainty and to overestimate our capabilities to deal with them.	1	2	3	4	5
Willingness to learn continually	Not at all		To some extent		To a great extent
We are willing to challenge our ways of working.	1	2	3	4	5
We are critical about our ways of managing risk and uncertainty.	1	2	3	4	5
Changing our ways of working is not considered an acknowledgment of incompetence.	1	2	3	4	5

Scoring: Add the numbers. If you score higher than 9 in each category, your project is ready for resilience. If you score 9 or lower in a category, you may wish to re-assess your approach to project management.

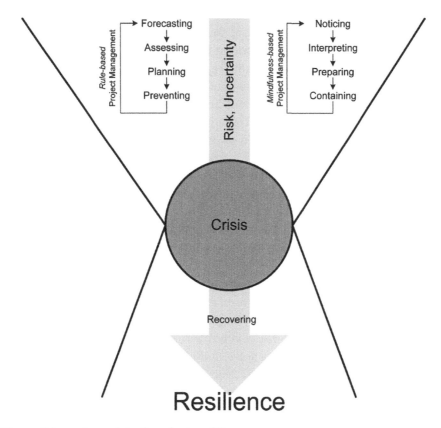

Figure 2.1   A model of project resilience

We run projects that are risky, uncertain and complex, in varying degrees. In environments that are complex, in which points of failure can quickly 'snowball' into crises, one may simply be reactive, catching up with adversity. Nevertheless, most projects succumb to a 'death by a thousand cuts'. Their performance does not collapse suddenly but gradually, with ample opportunity for a project leader to intervene, in advance of risk and uncertainty causing significant harm.

Putting complexity aside, modern project management bodies of knowledge tend to assume a world of risk where past occurrences can inform the future. The underlying rationale is that risk can be 'designed out' of a project by probabilistic, deterministic planning tools, enforced and applied in a consistent manner. Uncertainty plays a much smaller part in this logic. At the centre of such rule-based project management is the pre-loading and automation of fixed responses, based on a past-informed future. A rule-based approach is fundamentally Taylorist [1, 2]. Rules are put in place to pre-plan the future-based actions of forecasting, assessing and scheduling with the express purpose of prevention (see Figure 2.1). Human cognition – as a potential source of error – is being replaced by these pre-planned actions. A benefit of this approach is consistency of action (and we do fully acknowledge the benefits), but they are not without limitations. An 'autopilot' may enable managers to deal with common problems quickly and consistently but may struggle with effective responses to novelty and ambiguity.

In contrast to a rule-based way of working – one that assumes human cognition is fallible and thus a source of error – mindfulness-based project management (see Figure 2.1) puts situated human cognition at the forefront. Mindfulness ' … to a particular situation is not an attempt to make the best choice from available options but to create options' [3, p. 114].

> … [It] involves the combination of ongoing scrutiny of existing expectations, continuous refinement and differentiation of expectations based on newer experiences, willingness and capability to invent new expectations that make sense of unprecedented events, a more nuanced appreciation of context and ways to deal with it, and identification of new dimensions of context that improve foresight and current functioning. [4, p. 32]

In a state of mindfulness, people's experiences are sensitive to their environment and they feel in the present moment. Mindful projects have distinctive capabilities to anticipate, contain and bounce back from risk, but foremost is the ability to respond effectively to uncertainties, characterised by ambiguity and novelty.

WHAT THE LITERATURE SAYS ABOUT …
Mindfulness

The concept of mindfulness has provided us with the greatest inspiration for this book. A discrete body of research on High Reliability Organisations (HROs) emerged in the 1980s when the 'Berkeley Group' became concerned with organisations that repeatedly perform activities with 'high hazard' technologies but experience very few errors and incidents [5, 6]. Reliability from this perspective is regarded as a 'dynamic non-event' [7], which is not automatically attained, but has to be actively accomplished every day.

Much of this work on High Reliability Organisations focuses on the concept of mindfulness. Mindfulness is a well-established construct in social psychology literature and consists of four dimensions: *Alertness to Distinction, Openness to Novelty, Orientation in the Present,* and *Awareness of Multiple Perspectives* [3]. Mindfulness involves the continuous creation of new categories and openness to new information. When mindful, people's experiences are sensitive to their environment and feel in the present moment [8]. Similarly, the equally powerful yet destructive phenomenon of *mindlessness* involves: entrapment in old categories, automatic behaviour that precludes attending to new signals and actions that operate from a single perspective. When individuals succumb to automatic thought processes and act mindlessly, they often miss vital information.

Drawing on HRO literature, five organisational characteristics can be identified that are reliability-enhancing: *Preoccupation with Failure, Reluctance to Simplify, Sensitivity to Operations, Commitment to Resilience,* and *Deference to Expertise.* The concept of Preoccupation with Failure characterises a constant 'chronic unease' [9] about potential (small) errors. It draws people's attention (partially away from 'blinding' successes) towards the potential of catastrophic failure. People are continuously looking out for 'weak signals' [10] – signs of failure or deviations from a planned change that may cascade into a crisis. The reporting and sharing of weak signals is encouraged and incentivised. Near-misses and errors are used as learning opportunities and shared freely.

The constant look-out for weak signals is complemented by the second characteristic – *Reluctance to Simplify.* It counters people's tendency to normalise and ignore weak signals. It assumes that failure is not the result of a single, simple, cause. Weak signals are not seen as isolated, controllable, risks but as systemic failures that require a strong response. Nuanced appreciation of such systemic risk is required. People are encouraged not to jump to conclusions, to be sceptical and show constant doubt about simplified conclusions. Assumptions are challenged by evaluation from a variety of (cross-functional) perspectives. The aim of *Reluctance to Simplify* is to challenge engrained assumptions and to foster a more nuanced interpretation of failure.

Sensitivity to Operations relates to an organisational ability to remain close to where failure happens. 'Real-time' information exchange about failure and the ability of people to merge pieces of information to understand the 'big picture' of an operation (or project) is paramount. 'Knowing' how a situation unfolds requires fast and un-bureaucratic communication and the imagination to look beyond single weak signals in isolation.

Whereas *Preoccupation with Failure, Reluctance to Simplify and Sensitivity to Operations* characterise an increased awareness and nuanced appreciation of failure (indeed, an anticipation of failure), *Commitment to Resilience* and *Deference to Expertise* offer two principles for containing uncertainty. The ability to cope with, and successfully bounce back from, failure is associated with *Commitment to Resilience.* Those who are close to the problem and can enact a first-response to contain failure need to be encouraged and motivated to do so swiftly and competently. An increased 'response repository' through training and investment in skills, enabled by a widened responsibility and accountability, is at the forefront of establishing resilience here.

Nevertheless, mindful organising needs to be exercised by those closest to and most knowledgeable about the problem and its solution(s). Expertise needs to be drawn upon irrespective of organisational prestige, silo mentality, ego, or hierarchical divisions. *Deference to Expertise* implies that expertise is valued more than hierarchy. Rank and status are subordinated to knowledge and experience.

HROs have distinctive capabilities to anticipate, contain and bounce back from weak signals of failure. This is an acknowledgement both that they are not error-free and that neither can errors be designed out of a system. The unique characteristic of an HRO is that failure does not disable it but keeps it functioning. There is now a plethora of literature applying the basic notions and concepts of HRO design in, for example, schools [11], software firms [12] and railways [13]. Nevertheless, high reliability organising in projects has received surprisingly little attention.

Rule- and mindfulness-based ways of managing projects seem to have an uneasy co-existence. In the extreme, rule-based project management excludes any form of flexible thinking that could deal with uncertainties. Vice versa, mindfulness in its extreme would preclude any form of structure and consistent action. A 'true' state of resilience can indeed be achieved by targeting risks – efficiently – by enforcing rules and procedures that cover repeated occurrences of past threats, while also providing mindful capabilities that challenge the status quo of rule-based behaviour and facilitate the situated management of uncertainties efficiently and effectively.

Both archetypes of project management – rule- and mindfulness-based – have been applied in various contexts with greater or lesser degrees of success. Let us look at a case unlike any other that might trigger our imagination about resilience and give us a deeper understanding of what this means in a complex environment.

A 'Project' without Parallels

We could have chosen from a whole range of cases to provide a compelling insight into rule- and mindfulness-based approaches to managing adversity in a project. The Fall of France in 1940 at the hands of Nazi Germany offers a compelling insight into the two archetypes of managing risk and uncertainty, as these approaches stood in direct competition with each other in the most dramatic way possible.

The defeat of France in May–June 1940 was one of the great surprises of the twentieth century. The disparity between the French and German forces was staggering, yet the weaker party prevailed and Germany inflicted one of the 'strangest' defeats in military history. The reason for the defeat of France in 1940 lends itself to a renewed analysis from a project management perspective, given that the reasons for success and failure have real parallels to major project successes and failures in modern times.

10–15 May 1940: 'We Are Beaten; We Have Lost The Battle'

On 15 May 1940, Winston Churchill, still in bed, was called by Paul Reynaud, the French Prime Minister:

> *He spoke in English, and evidently under stress. 'We have been defeated.'*
> *As I did not immediately respond he said again: 'We are beaten; we have*
> *lost the battle.' I said: Surely it can't have happened so soon? But he*
> *replied: 'The front is broken near Sedan; they are pouring through in*
> *great numbers with tanks and armoured cars.' [14, p. 9]*

Only five days earlier, on 10 May, six German armies attacked the Low Countries (Holland, Belgium, Luxembourg) and crossed the river Meuse – at Sedan and Dinant, two small French towns. The plan for the invasion of France, code-named 'Fall Gelb' (Operation Yellow) was not the physical destruction of the French Army but, rather, the collapse of their morale and, subsequently, the military defeat of France [15]. The '*Oberkommando des Heeres*' (OKH) (German High Command) was convinced that a long drawn out war could not be won given the strength of the French Army and the logistical shortcomings on the German side [15]. Hence, after a series of unconvincing operational plans bearing strong similarities to the Schlieffen plan used in 1914, and postponements of the offensive due to security leakages and weather, the Manstein plan (named after Lieutenant General Erich von Manstein) was backed by Adolf Hitler and operationalised – they called it the '*Sichelschnitt*' (cut of the sickle). The directive, produced on 24 February, solved the long-disputed question of where the emphasis of the attack should be. In contrast to the original plan, it was not to be in the North with Army Group B, who might have bypassed the Maginot line (a mighty line of fortifications constructed along France's borders with Germany and Italy). Instead, Army Group B was allocated the role of a 'matador's cloak' [16, 17] to lure the bulk of the French forces into Belgium, away from the new point of attack, and into a trap where they would be encircled and destroyed.

The weight of the armoured drive shifted south to the upper Meuse (see Figure 2.2), a river in the area of Sedan at the outer edge of the Maginot line, the weakest point in the French front line. Once across the Meuse, Army Group A, with 41,000 vehicles, planned to swing westwards (the cut of the sickle) and thrust to the channel coast, resulting in the encirclement of the bulk of the French forces and their allies [18]. Army Group C, with only 18 divisions, was left to defend the 'Siegfried Line' (a line of defensive forts and tank defences) and launch diversionary attacks on the Maginot Line [19].

The French strategy in contrast, relied on the Dyle Breda plan. The strong Seventh Army, under General Giraud, was placed to the North. In collaboration with the British Expeditionary Force and General Blanchard's First Army, the Allied forces were supposed to move to the River Dyle to absorb the weight of the German attack. General Corap's Ninth Army was to occupy the area along the Meuse just north of Sedan. Below Sedan, occupying the gap between Sedan and the start of the Maginot Line, General Huntzinger was placed with his Second Army. The divisions under his command were of mediocre quality because a German attack through the thickly forested area of the Ardennes was considered unlikely and, if such an attack should occur, the French would have sufficient time to reinforce [20].

On 10 May, the German forces launched their offensive. General Heinz Guderian's XIX Panzer corps punched through the southern end of the Maginot line and successfully crossed the river Meuse at Sedan on 13 May. Meanwhile, General Hoth, with his 7th Panzer Division, under the leadership of the enigmatic Erwin Rommel, overcame the defences at Dinant and established a bridgehead on the same day. The successful crossing of the Meuse on 13 May, just three days after the beginning of the campaign, sealed the fate of the French Army.

The true extent of the defeat may be read in the French and Allied losses. The German casualty rate was 156,492 (killed 27,074; wounded 111,034; missing 18,384). In contrast the French were estimated to have lost 2,190,000 (killed 90,000; wounded 200,000; missing/prisoners 1,900,000) [21]. In just six weeks, the German Armed Forces went on to bring a military juggernaut (casualty rates: British 68,111; Dutch 9,779; Belgian 23,350) to its knees. The defeat of the Allies was so profound that it demands an explanation.

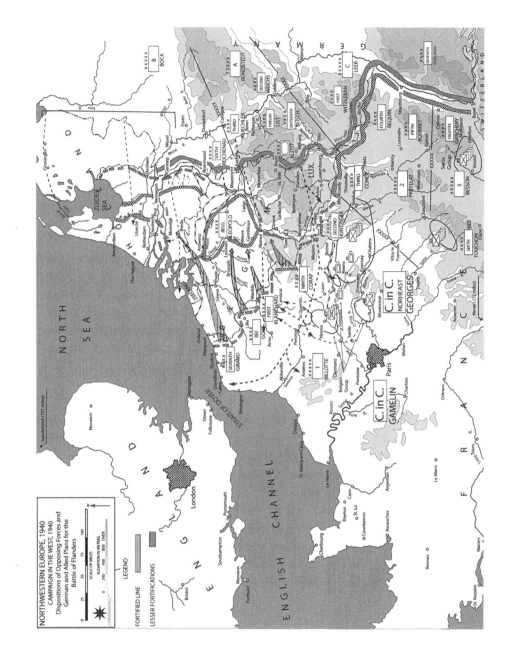

Figure 2.2
Disposition and opposing forces, May 1940

David versus Goliath

The military disposition of both armies clearly favoured the French. The French and her allies engaged in total 134 divisions: the French had 79 divisions plus 13 fortress divisions and there were an additional 22 Belgian, 10 British and 10 Dutch divisions. Hitler could rely on 135 divisions [14]. In quality, the divisions varied on both sides. The Allies were in possession of around 3,000 tanks, most of which outgunned their German counterparts (2,400 tanks) and provided greater protection. France also had more artillery pieces than Germany (a ratio of 3 to 2). Only in the air were the allied forces outclassed by the German Luftwaffe [20].

Given the French superiority of arms on the ground, one might be tempted to attribute the defeat to mobile tank warfare, introduced by the Germans. However, although there is some truth in the idea that the French only used their armoured divisions to support their infantry (and this only in a 'drip-feed' fashion), they also had the capability to stop an amphibious river crossing, considered to be one of the most difficult undertakings in warfare: 'Whatever the advantages for the Germans, however, the campaign was not a "walk through the sun" for them' [22, p. 4].

By the same token, the often-credited doctrine of armoured 'Blitzkrieg' (lightning war) also needs to be put in perspective [23]. Only 10 German divisions were fully armoured. The majority of the German Forces relied on soldiers on foot, supported by horses. Hence, an armoured lightning war would have been ill conceived: ' … particularly since Guderian's doctrine about tank warfare was neither fully understood nor fully approved by his commanders, and Rommel's idiosyncratic doctrine was at odds with it' [24, p. 449]. In those cases where the infantry and armour were supported by tactical air support, the impact of the Luftwaffe on the French fortifications (the Maginot line) can best be described as minimal, especially in the Sedan sector [23].

The morale of the French Army, especially in the initial stages of the Meuse crossing and despite the later rout, also does not suffice as the primary reason for the ultimate collapse of the front around Sedan. Multiple accounts [e.g. 22, 24] underline the tenacity and courage with which the French and Belgian defenders along the Meuse opposed the German invaders [21].

We need to understand the 'why' of the final outcome, given the setup of a French Goliath versus a German David. How could the Germans have ' … outfought the French tactically and outsmarted them strategically … '? [22, p. 4].

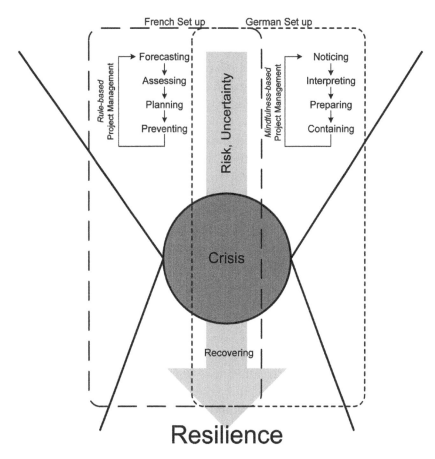

Figure 2.3   **Focus on rule-based and mindfulness-based project management**

'Bataille Conduit and Colmatage' versus 'Auftragstaktik'

Let us begin with the overall manner of waging war (see Figure 2.3). France, being reliant on a largely 'Citizen'-army, focused predominantly on determining when, where and how the Germans would attack, and controlling every situation by executing a different plan. This was very much a rule-based approach. The Germans were able to deploy a professional army, although in an ad-hoc fashion. Some planning was carried out but ultimately, it was down to the 'boots on the ground' to manage a rapidly-changing situation, based on the exploitation of human situated cognition – of mindfulness.

From the French perspective, the approach to preventing the Germans from invading their country was predominantly driven by a rule-based approach to managing adversity (see Figure 2.3) which was top-down, centralised, and methodical. Encapsulated by the idea of *'la bataille conduit'* (methodical battle), this gave the French forces little freedom to act. With the promise that any attack would be stopped by massive firepower, improvisation was to be avoided and all steps were meticulously prepared in advance [14]. If the worst happened and the enemy was close to breaking through the French defences, the only French response was to plug the gap with reinforcements (*'colmatage'*). The strategic aim of the French High Command was to provide a defensive advantage by initially absorbing any enemy attack, providing an opportunity to counterattack and switch to the offensive. However, their strategic preference for an operation based on a single scenario assumption left them vulnerable to any unexpected moves by the Germans. 'The French Military knew what kind of war they expected to fight. They also knew where they expected (and wanted) to fight: in Belgium' [14, p. 25].

At the heart of the German approach was the autonomous deployment of Panzer forces at an operational level [23] – *'Auftragstaktik'* (mission oriented leadership), a doctrinal approach very much relying on the deployment of mindful capabilities (see Figure 2.3). Mission oriented leadership was characterised by the military commanders providing their subordinate leaders with an understanding of the intent behind orders and how these fit into the strategic perspective. Operationally and tactically, these subordinate leaders were equipped with wide ranging independence and freedom of execution, but within the boundaries of standard operating procedures.

The role of operational independence was fulfilled by the provisionally formed *'Panzergruppe'* Kleist, whose sole target was to cross the river Meuse and exploit any breakthrough as a springboard for an envelopment of the French Forces. Such operational independence could not have been carried out without logistical abundance and independence, as pointed out by Oberst Zeitzler: 'If ever the success of an operation depended on supplies, that is the case with our operation' [25, p. 161].

This operational and logistical independence went hand in hand with an awareness of the importance of crossing the Meuse rapidly and of the vulnerability of the operation to failure at that point. It was imperative that the river be successfully crossed at any place possible, no matter what. Because of the significance, and in order to cover for the eventuality of a failed crossing, three entire corps were committed to the Sedan sector.

Two Archetypes of Resilience Revisited

The battle of Sedan in 1940 offers a peculiar picture. If we see it as two project teams in competition, both are equipped with rationales that could guarantee success: 'Thanks largely to an infatuation with a mythical Blitzkrieg, we are far too quick to dismiss the methodical battle as an example of stupid doctrine' [26, p. 114].

These two ways – French rule-based versus German mindfulness-based – are fundamentally different styles and both offer advantages that, in the light of the superior resources on the French side, should not have allowed the breakthrough at Sedan. Indeed, detailed planning associated with the deployment of far superior resources should, in principle, have tipped the balance in favour of the French. Nevertheless, as with any project, the question is less about the key resources than how they are applied in practice and how they are utilised to meet the overall objective. Regarding the application of rule- and mindfulness-based project management, let us consider:

- Time – What is the effect of time on processes, functioning, behaviour and performance?
- Team – How do groups of people in temporary organisational systems resolve issues of uncertainty and risk? [based on 27–30]
- Task – What kind of tasks do temporary organisational forms perform?

Time

How did the French make sense of time? Their approach to engaging with the upcoming German attack was set by prior expectations. These expectations and the planning which went with them added to a form of 'tunnel vision', a restricted understanding that the Germans would attack through Belgium. Alternative frames of reality were blocked out, despite on-going concerns about the unpreparedness of the Sedan front [31]. Once the offensive was under way, the French Generals were not sufficiently close to operations to realise in real-time that their plans did not apply to the situation at hand:

> *Gamelin's headquarters were as far back as Vincennes, virtually in the Paris suburbs, because the Commander-in-Chief felt he needed to be closer to the Government than to his own Army. His field commander, Alphonse Georges … was based in La Ferte, 35 miles east of Paris, but spent much of his time at his residence 12 miles from the capital. [32, p. 56]*

Crucial information that came to the attention of the High Command was already out of date upon their receiving it, at times by several hours. Even when they did receive information, they failed to see that anything was going awry. This was typified by reports they received from the front, massively underestimating the situation. For example, General Huntzinger's staff reported 'There has been a rather serious hitch at Sedan'[22].

This offers an insight into the self-inflicted deception and denial which was going on. Information about successes, for example against the 2nd Panzer Division which was struggling to reach its staging area on time and was bogged down by French artillery, was amplified. In contrast, information about retreats, initially carried out in a planned and methodical way, was downplayed to the extent that Georges signalled Gamelin at midnight on 13 May 'Here we are all calm' [24, p. 411].

The French fixation on a single theatre of battle in the North, lack of sensitivity to the state of defence in the Sedan sector and being cut off from information, coupled with ignorance and the premature commitment of reserves based on expectations, meant that, for the Allies, the battle for France was fought in something of a vacuum. Only the opportunistic intervention of individual divisions could have turned the tide. However, bound by a top-down approach, decisions to counterattack were taken late or not at all. Furthermore, where opportunities emerged to counter the establishment of a German bridgehead, logistical dependencies prevented a quick reaction. For example, the mobilisation of counterattacks by the 55th Division, which was responsible for the Sedan sector, was bogged down by the layers of hierarchy through which orders had to find their way. It took a staggering nine hours to mobilise a counterattack. By then, the situation on the ground had already changed considerably:

1900 hours: Telephone discussion between Grandsard and Lafontaine about attachment of additional infantry and tanks for a counterattack.

1930 hours: Telephone discussion between Grandsard and Lafontaine about moving command post of 55th Division.

After 1930 hours: Movement of 55th's command post. Lafontaine meets Labarthe in Chemery.

After 1930 hours: Lieutenant Colonel Cachou, who was the deputy Chief of Staff of the Xth Corps, meets Labarthe in Chemery. Approves Labarthe's decision not to move north.

After 1930 hours: Cachou meets Lafontaine east of Chemery. Informs him of Labarthe's decision.

After 1930 hours: Lafontaine calls Grandsard to discuss counterattack.

2200–2300 hours: Lafontaine definitely learns that the 205th Regiment and 4th Tank Battalion are being attached to the 55th Division.

2400 hours: Lafontaine departs for Xth Corps command post.

0130 hours: Chaligne learns that counterattack would consist of two infantry regiments and two tank battalions.

0300 hours: Lafontaine returns to Chemery without having reached Xth Corps.

0415 hours: Lafontaine issues order for counterattack [22, p. 260].

The well-prepared plans gave a false impression of what was 'supposed' to be happening and when. Events were expected to unfold as the plan predicted, yet what was happening in the field told a different story. The discrepancy between expectations and reality could not readily be compensated for as real-time updates were either downplayed or simply took too long to be relayed between the commanders and the front line.

In contrast, the Germans considered time as organic. Their strategic planning for the invasion of France was superseded by the operational necessities and uncertainties. A river needs to be crossed quickly, no matter what, and everything else depends on its outcome. This may sound haphazard and reckless, but detailed planning of the 'when' and 'how' was replaced by 'whatever' was operationally necessary, given the unfolding events on the ground. The initially conceived plan of 'what should be done when' was no longer the overriding factor. Instead, responses 'in the moment' meant that timely decisions and actions were paramount.

Officers such as Guderian and Rommel 'led from the front', capturing time as it unfolded, racing between their headquarters and the developing events [14]. Rommel (7th Panzer, Dinant), for example, tried to be always in the 'picture' of developing events by crossing the Meuse with one of the first wave of assault teams. His scepticism about initial success turned into a curiosity about what was going on and a decision only to share such oversight with his chief of staff if necessary.

Team

The French doctrine was characterised by strong, centralised, hierarchical, decision making. This is unsurprising given that those executing orders – mostly conscripts – had little or no experience and were given only limited training to make decisions on their own. As team members were often allocated to areas of operation and to regiments they were unfamiliar with, there was little bonding and unfamiliarity about their environment prevailed. Such inconsistency is often associated with modern projects, in which resources are parachuted in for a limited period of time, initially oblivious of the team context. The teams – platoons, regiments, and battalions – were expected to function by following the orders provided, context free. This is the classic 'command and control' style. Orders were stripped of the 'why', and this could not be replaced by the (lack of) experience of those that had to execute them.

The German approach, in stark contrast, focused on the development of internally cohesive, well-equipped teams with an extraordinary response repository and independence to exercise that flexibility. Subordinate leaders were given, to a large extent, insights into the mission objectives and strategic ramifications, and a freedom in execution. For example, General Heinz Guderian (XIXth Panzer Corps, Sedan) later reflected: 'During the French campaign, I never received any further orders as to what I was to do once the bridgehead over the Meuse was captured. All of my decisions, until I reached the Atlantic seaboard at Abbeville, were taken by me alone' [33, p. 251].

Prior to Operation Yellow, teams of specialists were defined within Panzergruppe Kleist. They were kept together as much as possible and rehearsed a range of scenarios, ranging from amphibious landings to urban warfare. These kinds of 'Tiger Teams' were given experience of the context of warfare through rehearsals, and their performance was driven by orders from superiors who were very 'close' to them.

Task

The French frontline soldiers were tasked with countering a German attack. However, using the example of the 147th Division, their preparations included constant digging and fortifying, with little emphasis on the practical aspects of combat: 'Many of the soldiers in the 147th knew their responsibilities in the smallest detail, but their skills for defending fortresses or firing machine guns were useless in regular infantry units' [22, p. 127].

Their preparation – digging and fortifying – left little time to prepare the French soldiers for actual fighting. It was – wrongly – assumed that giving orders to the front line soldiers would compensate for the lack of knowing 'why' and 'how'. Execution of tasks was expected to be done in isolation of the specific context. This would not have been such a problem if the orders matched the unfolding situation. Unfortunately, that was not the case, and along the Sedan sector, backed into a corner with orders that no longer made sense, the French Forces took their own initiative and retreated in the hope of receiving fresh orders to form another coherent front further back.

With the French very much task-oriented, the Germans followed a slightly different approach of goal-orientation, in which the achievements of objectives superseded the specificity of execution. Such goal-orientation can only work if teams are prepared and ready to carry out any task necessary to accomplish the given aims. Their flexibility was such that not only did they provide their own logistics but they also made sure that a range of specialists (e.g. the Grossdeutschland Regiment) were immediately available to adapt to a changing situation.

The German forces applied a risky and potentially costly strategy of mindfulness. With speed as the most important factor, the crossing of the Meuse received operational preference. Such intent was carried out with a specialised, yet operationally and logistically independent, force. Methodology and operating procedures – rule-based management – played less of a role because of the specially trained units' ability to achieve the intent of crossing a river and establishing a bridgehead. This subsequently enabled the encirclement of the French Forces and this logic was embedded in their thinking. Rules did not have to be tightly controlled and deviation from a method for the benefit of achieving the operational aim was not only allowed but encouraged.

The French applied a supposedly more certain strategy of not allowing French front-line soldiers and officers to think on their feet. Orders were relayed from the top to the front line, to be executed without question. This does make sense given the largely conscript army whose soldiers would not have the knowledge and experience to think and act flexibly enough under such difficult conditions. The ultimate breakdown of the rule-based approach here was down to delayed or absent communication and the lack of preparation for the scenario that actually unfolded.

More than anything else, this happened because France and its allies misjudged what Germany planned to do. If leaders in the Allied governments had anticipated the German offensive through the Ardennes, even as a worrisome contingency, it is almost inconceivable that France would have been defeated when and as it was. It is more conceivable that the outcome would have been not France's defeat but Germany's and, possibly, a French victory parade on the Unter den Linden in Berlin. [24, p. 5]

The Temptation of Rule-based Project Management

On one hand, a rule-based approach to project management offers greater efficiency, accountability and stability (or, perhaps, the illusion of it). On the other hand, a situated cognition-based approach to risk and uncertainty offers the required flexibility to deal with situations that deviate from the norm. And there is the problem. In projects we often start with a rule-based approach, like the French did. We plan, set up procedures and run our projects the 'right' way. It is a form of 'dogmatism', the tendency to lay down principles as incontrovertibly true, without consideration of the evidence or the opinions of others [34].

Such dogmatism, developed over time, may undermine organisational readiness when the situation demands a different response. Why communicate extensively if normality is assumed? Such dogmatism is entrenched by long periods of planning and the absence of failure. This sends the message that the system is working, reinforcing faith in the process. The more we believe that plans will unfold as predicted, the less we prepare and ready ourselves for uncertainty, for a situation that has not been anticipated. This diminishes the capability for intuitive responses. It is not surprising that the French held on to their expectations until it was too late.

Even the Germans, after their stunning success in overcoming their French foe, gradually succumbed to a move away from a mindfulness-based approach to a more rigid rule-based form of management: 'The rapidity of the German victory [in France] had created a dangerous hubris among the German military, and on the part of Hitler himself a fatal conviction that he was a military genius who could never be wrong. This was to prove his ultimate undoing' [14, p. 237].

A stark example of this was the battle of Kursk in July–August 1943. Hitler gave his generals little leeway in planning this battle and what they produced was a transparent scheme that the Soviet senior planners easily anticipated. Imagination played a lesser role. The focus on the repetition of previous schemes of warfare, the obsession of Hitler to plan every move in detail – similar to the French in 1940 – and the constant delay in launching the offensive (e.g. because of the deployment of new tank designs) turned the battle of Kursk into a methodical and inflexible endeavour that was countered by the Soviet Union even before it started. As a result, after Kursk the Soviets were more powerful than the Germans and their allies on the Eastern Front. In that sense, initiative changed hands at Kursk and operational failure was accelerated by the lack of manpower and increasingly centralised, rule-based, past-driven decision-making by the German High Command and Hitler:

> It was one of the great ironies of the War that as Hitler, frustrated and disillusioned from being unable to secure victory over the USSR proceeded to deprive his commanders of their independence and centralized more and more the conduct of the war into his own hands, Stalin was moving in the opposite direction, seeking to encourage within the Red Army that very operational flexibility and independence in decision-making in the field that had been responsible for Germany's victories in the first three years of the conflict. [35, p. 109]

In projects, the question is not whether to adopt a fully rule-based or mindfulness-based approach, because they both have their advantages and disadvantages. We often see organisations tempted to start a project with a rule-based approach, or to shift gradually to one characterised by reducing situated human cognition and a greater focus on compliance to rules and procedures. Does that automatically imply that this approach is superior, despite the inability of the French Forces to make it work? Well, yes and no. Rule-based management is a more fruitful approach in environments that unfold very much in linear, predictable ways, informed by risk. The major benefit of traditional, rule-based project management is one of efficiency. Less experienced resources – similar to the French citizen army – can be deployed. The rationale is that these can quite easily be brought in as required on project-based contracts and are more substitutable (and cheaper), but this situation needs strong control and monitoring. In this respect, the more flexible form of deploying situated human cognition may well be wasteful. Capability to deal with risk and uncertainty may remain underutilised, with people prepared for the worst and ready to respond, yet with only a fraction of these capabilities being deployed at any given time.

This rule-based approach – with its premise of efficiency – only works if project plans are adjusted effectively according to the unfolding risk and uncertainty and if this is done quickly enough to deal with complexity. In this respect, not just compliance but real-time communication and the ability of project managers to change their plans are of paramount importance. A strongly hierarchical structure can be a hindrance to updating plans as communication has to bridge more levels of responsibility and thus may not allow the spontaneity in decision-making necessary. In addition, the greater the effort that goes into detailed plans, the more managers are wedded to them. Their expectations can be driven more and more by what they (want to) expect and not by what is actually happening.

A mindfulness-based approach is more suited to managing projects characterised by uncertainty. The major benefit of this as a management approach is that it provides greater awareness, more nuanced appreciation of changing circumstances and greater flexibility in containing uncertainty. Rules are ill-suited to deal with novelty and ambiguity. Not so our minds. As flawed as they may be, they offer an amazing flexibility to deal with uncertainty, a feat no rule-based system can ever achieve.

What many managers have failed to appreciate is that human variability offers a way of providing the flexibility necessary to manage uncertainty. It is increasingly recognised that a wider perspective on dealing with risk and uncertainty is required if one wants to look beyond what has repeatedly happened in the past [13, 36]. This has led to an acknowledgement that rule-based management is beneficial, as long as it allows mindfulness to flourish. 'True' resilience in a project is most likely the outcome of some rule-based management, yet with leeway to deploy the human mind to accommodate novelty and ambiguity as an outcome of uncertainty.

Consequently, in most successful modern projects, one can find a mix of both rule-based and mindfulness-based approaches to managing risk and uncertainty. It is the ability to impose control, yet offer enough 'space' to mindfully manage uncertainty that goes beyond what one can predict and plan for in detail. Furthermore, resilient projects are those which are reluctant – in the absence of failure or because of failure – to give in to the temptation to impose ever more adherence to rules and procedures. The following chapters go into more detail on what obstacles we may need to overcome in order to be mindful. Our subsequent ability to manage uncertainty better will lessen the chances of our project being derailed by adversity, a highly desirable and worthwhile outcome.

Reflection

To what extent does your project focus adhere to one or the other mode of management in your project? For each item, select one box only that best reflects your conclusion.

Time			Neutral			
The project is pre-planned in its entirety.						We allow things to happen and react to those.
We can anticipate all risks.						We acknowledge that the project is inherently unknown territory.
Time unfolds in a linear, predictable, fashion.						Time is messy, unpredictable, ambiguous and unknown.
Team			**Neutral**			
We follow a centralised approach to management.						We follow a de-centralised approach to management.
Consistency of action is paramount.						We provide people with the freedom to act
We value hierarchy over experience.						We value experience over rank.
Task			**Neutral**			
Compliance is most important.						Goal-orientation is most important.
Tasks are executed according to predefined actions.						Tasks are executed according to the actual situation.
Obedience drives the execution of tasks						Responsibility and empowerment drive task execution.

Scoring: You may tend towards one or the other extreme or simply find yourself in the middle of these extremes of the two project management approaches. Please consider what benefits your current approach entails, and whether a modified approach might make sense in that particular piece of work.

References

1. Butler, B.S. and P.H. Gray, Reliability, Mindfulness, and Information Systems. *MIS Quarterly*, 2006. 30(2): p. 211–24.

2. Morgan, G., *Images of Organization*. 1986, Beverly Hills, CA: Sage Publications.

3. Langer, E.J., *The Power of Mindful Learning*. 1997, Reading, MA: Addison-Wesley.

4. Weick, K. and K. Sutcliffe, *Managing the Unexpected: Resilient Performance in an Age of Uncertainty*. 2nd edition 2007, San Francisco: Jossey-Bass.

5. Rochlin, G.I., Defining 'High Reliability' Organizations in Practice: A Taxonomic Prologue, in *New Challenges in Understanding Organizations*, K.H. Roberts (ed.), 1993, Macmillan: New York. 11–32.

6. Roberts, K.H., Some Characteristics of One Type of High Reliability Organization. *Organization Science*, 1990. 1(2): p. 160–76.

7. Weick, K. and K. Sutcliffe, *Managing the Unexpected: Resilient Performance in an Age of Uncertainty*. 2001, San Francisco: Jossey Bass.

8. Langer, E.J., *Mindfulness*. 1989, Camb. MA.: Perseus Publishing.

9. Reason, J., *Human Error*. 1990, Cambridge: Cambridge University Press.

10. Weick, K.E. and K.H. Roberts, Collective Mind in Organizations: Heedful Interrelating on Flight Decks. *Administrative Science Quarterly*, 1993. 38(3): p. 357–81.

11. Reynolds, D., S. Stringfield, and E. Schaffer, The High Reliability Schools Project. Some Preliminary Results and Analyses, in *School Improvement: International Perspectives*, J. Crispeels and A. Harris (eds), 2006, Routledge: London. p. 56–76.

12. Vogus, T.J. and T.M. Welbourne, Structuring for High Reliability: HR Practices and Mindful Processes in Reliability-Seeking Organizations. *Journal of Organizational Behavior*, 2003. 24(7): p. 877–903.

13. Busby, J.S., Failure to Mobilize in Reliability-Seeking Organizations: Two Cases from the UK Railway. *Journal of Management Studies*, 2006. 43(6): p. 1375–93.

14. Jackson, J., *The Fall of France*. 2003, New York: Oxford University Press.

15. Deighton, L., *From the Rise of Hitler to the Fall of Dunkirk*. 2007, London: Pimlico.

16. Hart, L., *The Liddell Hart Memoirs, 1895–1938*. 1965, New York: G.P. Putnam's Sons.

17. Caddick-Adams, P., *The Battle for France and Flanders Sixty Years On*, B. Bond and M. Taylor (eds), 2001, Barnsley, S. Yorkshire: Pen & Sword.

18. Warner, P., *The Battle of France, 1940*. 1990, London: Cassell & Co.

19. Bjorge, G.J., *Decisiveness. Combined Arms in Battle Since 1939*, R.J. Spiller (ed.), 1992, Fort Leavenworth, Kansas: US Army Command and General Staff College Press.

20. Sheppard, A., *France 1940: Blitzkrieg in the West*. 1990, Oxford: Osprey Publishing.

21. Horne, A., *To Lose a Battle*. 1969, London: Penguin.
22. Doughty, R.A., *The Breaking Point: Sedan and the Fall of France*. 1990, Hamden: Archon.
23. Frieser, K.-H., *The Blitzkrieg Legend: The 1940 Campaign in the West*. 2005, Annapolis, MD: Naval Institute Press.
24. May, E.R., *Strange Victory: Hitler's Conquest of France*. 2009, London: I.B. Tauris & Co.
25. Graf Kielmansegg, *Panzer zwischen Warschau und Atlantik* 1941, Berlin: Die Wehrmacht.
26. Kiesling, E.C., The Fall of France: Lessons of the 1940 Campaign. *Defence Studies*, 2003. 3(1): p. 109–23.
27. Bakker, R.M., Taking Stock of Temporary Organizational Forms: A Systematic Review and Research Agenda. *International Journal of Management Reviews*, 2010. 12: p. 466–86.
28. Lundin, R.A. and A. Soederholm, A Theory of the Temporary Organisation. *Scandinavian Journal of Management*, 1995. 11(4): p. 437–55.
29. Lundin, R.A. and R.S. Steinthorsson, Studying Organizations as Temporary. *Scandinavian Journal of Management*, 2003. 19: p. 233–50.
30. Raab, J., et al., Structure in Temporary Organizations, in *Temporary Organizations: Prevalence, Logic and Effectiveness*, P. Kenis, Janowicz-Panjaitan, and B. Crambre (eds), 2009, Edward Elgar: Cheltenham, UK.
31. Burne, A.H., The Second Sedan. *The RUSI Journal*, 1946. 91(564): p. 570–76.
32. Roberts, A., *The Storm of War: A New History of the Second World War*. 2009, London: Penguin.
33. Guderian, H., *Panzer Leader*. 2000, London: Penguin Classics.
34. Finkel, M., *On Flexibility: Recovery from Technological and Doctrinal Surprise on the Battlefield* 2011, Stanford: Stanford University Press.
35. Healy, M., *Zitadelle: The German Offensive Against the Kursk Salient 4–17 July 1943*. 2008, Brimscombe Port Stroud: The History Press.
36. Coutu, D.L., Sense and Reliability, in *Harvard Business Review*. 2003, Harvard Business School Publication Corp. p. 84–90.

Chapter 3
THE ART OF NOTICING

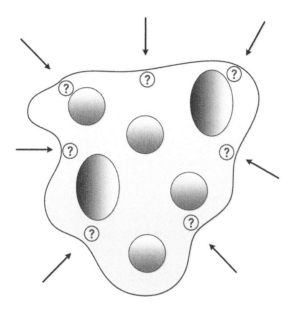

A project team can suddenly find itself facing the challenge of adversity. The lead-up to this can be ambiguous and subtle, and often there is little warning. It is useful to foster a keen state of awareness that recognises and anticipates emerging adversity, but trouble is often only visible when it unfolds and a response is required. This chapter provides some answers as to how risks can be noticed, if not necessarily forecast in the traditional way. It addresses the issues of: 'How can we foresee the future better?' 'How far we can look ahead?' and 'How we can keep an eye on uncertainty and complexity?'

The Lure of Certainty

On our road to 'notice more' risk, uncertainty and complexity, there are some obstacles. A central challenge is somewhat self-inflicted and lies with our way of thinking. We are naturally tempted to fall back on our ideas of a world of certainty because we tend to feel more comfortable with that. There are, though, a range of lures that limit our noticing.

Expectations of Normality

We want things to be fine. We would like the plan to unfold just as the schedule pinned to the wall shows that it should. We long for a continuous state of 'normality' and therefore perhaps it is not surprising that such longings lead us to ignore indications of failure. We may be surrounded by signs of potential adversity, yet because these do not fit our expectations, we tend to disregard them so that we and our stakeholders remain in a state of relative comfort.

Complacency

The assumption of normality is reinforced by periods of success. Success is characterised by the absence of failures. Such accomplishments in the past make us think that we can expect the same to continue into the future. We are increasingly focused on what has worked, rather than on what might go wrong. Hence, we may limit our attention with regards to signs of possible failure. Our minds are focused on what we want to see. We anticipate that this success will continue (and why not?) and any potential signs of looming adversity do not fit our expectations. This complacency means that we are more attentive to information that reinforces our confidence and less likely to pick up on small signs of trouble ahead.

Focusing on the Familiar

Even so, some of the messages may make it onto our 'radar' of noticing. We are more likely to take into account information we are familiar with. For example, if a potential problem looks similar to one we have encountered in the past, this familiarity helps us identify and make sense of it. Consequently, our attention may be drawn to those factors we are more accustomed to. Unfamiliar features, characterised by ambiguity, are more likely to be filtered from our attention.

Aiming at the Measurable

Filtering out the unfamiliar failures goes hand-in-hand with paying attention to the measurable and quantifiable. If a piece of information lacks specificity, that signifies ambiguity, and people have a tendency to blank it out. Hence, we might only take into consideration information about a failure which is unambiguous enough to be processed further, that is to say, to be managed. As a consequence, we might take our project into the unknown, only noticing or wanting to notice aspects of failure that are 'clear' enough to us and which we have experienced in the past. However, because we have a tendency only to notice what we expect to notice, our 'radar', especially for uncertainty, is often not as sensitive as we would like.

Negative Connotation

The term 'risk' is often understood as 'bad things happening'. The upside, 'opportunity', is far less commonly discussed. Who would believe adversity to be a 'good' thing? These negative connotations frame the discussion in a bad light, as the language used hints at the manager's inability to design all adversity out of a project in the first place. Looking out for something considered negative is uncomfortable and increases our reluctance to engage with it.

Fixation

When we are preoccupied with 'doing things', our capacity to look out for new signs of adversity is diminished. When we are fixated on – preoccupied with – what matters to us, we tend to lose the ability to detect other important information. Early detection of fixation is highly beneficial. When strongly preoccupied, our ability to notice failure significantly decreases even though later, with the benefit of hindsight, we may not understand how we didn't recognise the signs of impending difficulty.

Myopia

A fixation on getting things done, our expectation of normality and our focus on the tangible and measurable leads to a propensity to be 'short-sighted' – to look into the near future and ignore long-term scenarios. We may only take the short-term future into consideration, leaving us unprepared for what could lie beyond that limited horizon.

Key Enablers to the Art of Noticing

In the previous section we identified some of the behavioural shortcomings that limit our ability to notice, in particular, uncertainty. There is help, though! In the following sections, we provide an overview of 'what' one can do and 'how'. We elaborate on how to notice and, in particular, how to detect signs of adversity which are ambiguous and lack the specificity of risk. The key issue of noticing is – traditionally – one of living in the past and believing that the future will unfold as the past did. Worse, in the absence of failure we gradually reduce our awareness of the need to 'look out' for warning signs that are unfamiliar and immeasurable, yet which could provide us with an early warning that something is not right. So what does this mean in practice for the project manager?

Acknowledgement

In order to notice risk and uncertainty, one needs to understand the environment that is at stake – the project. Noticing risk and uncertainty without knowledge about the human, technical, organisational and environmental factors that determine the success of a project is comparable to trying to find a needle in a haystack without understanding the concept of a haystack. Therein lies the challenge. Projects are inherently risky, uncertain and complex. Any understanding of 'how it works' might be temporary, at best, and necessitates a knowledge of the project 'here-and-now' as well as the needs and wants of the multiple stakeholders.

So the first enabler of greater resilience is an acknowledgement that our world is not only risky, but uncertain and complex. It is a message – 'we do not necessarily know' – that is powerful and yet often unnerving, as it counters our longing for certainty and comfort.

Vigilance

Accepting this knowledge deficiency and the resulting perceived uncertainty should trigger an almost permanent state of unease. This unease stems from the project constantly being assailed by possible risk and uncertainty: every new action and activity is an opportunity for something to go wrong or to work out in an unexpected manner. This is not, though, a reason for project participants to panic. Rather, it is a reason to be alert and attuned to the possibility that any minor error, problem, or close call could be symptomatic of a flaw in the wider project system. Such events must be scrutinised with the 'big picture' in mind. What are the possible wider implications? What does it signify? What might its root cause be?

This means that the process of anticipation should never really cease, but ought to manifest itself in the project environment. This should result in heightened alertness for the project manager and the team. They must be alive to the vagaries of the project, not just in terms of variances in the overall schedule and budget but also in terms of the wider project system and its multiple interconnected aspects.

Freedom to be Vigilant

This sense of unease and the alertness to the signs of adversity it should inspire do not come out of thin air. What is required is space in the form of time to spend on spotting failure. Project managers who are preoccupied with administrative tasks may be less sensitive to any failure happening around them. They need to be given the freedom and opportunity to be on the lookout – permanently – and to ask potentially inconvenient questions. This involves spending time close to what is happening. Yet this is often not what we see project managers doing. Sometimes, organisational incentives and systems drive managers to focus on detailed reporting and ensuring adherence to the original plan. This is all well and good, of course, but execution with only limited alertness is like crossing a busy street with only one eye on the traffic. Relying on luck is a poor strategy.

Reporting Culture

It is not just down to the project manager to be on high alert. Adversity should be spotted throughout the project by the various participants. To create effective project awareness, though, adversity needs to be reported quickly and honestly. Organisational culture (and the lack of incentives) often means that 'bad news' is not passed on to others. Silo thinking and the negative connotations of such 'inconveniences' can prevent people from reporting failures, both small and large. When a failure occurs or once individuals suspect poor performance, they need to share this information confidently and in a timely manner, without the fear of being blamed or considered a troublemaker.

Cross-functional Teams

Complex projects are best run with the benefit of multiple perspectives. The richness of different views from a range of involved stakeholders offers the opportunity to augment one's own 'radar' for what might go wrong. Diversity here does not just cover gender, ethnicity and cultural background, but also the work background and expertise of participants. Taking on board the views of legal, commercial, finance, marketing, operations, procurement and HR, as well as those of technical representatives, brings in much more knowledge and insight. Every 'lookout' will be vigilant about the area he or she is familiar with and bringing them all together allows a wider sensitivity to what may go wrong or is going wrong. This does not imply, though, that multiple – often diverging – perceptions should be moulded into a single consensus view which consequently becomes anchored as a commitment. The purpose of cross-functional perspective is to provide a rich picture, often with contradictory views, to provoke further thinking and discussion. In this respect it is not really intended to enable simplification.

Intelligent Tools

Most project management tools are based on the rationale of turning a complex and uncertain environment into a single most likely future. Instead of challenging a project manager's assumptions, they often reinforce the illusion of certainty, providing single estimates which are turned into commitments and corresponding simple 'pass/fail' criteria. Rarely is the real world this straightforward.

Any risk management system should include mechanisms to look beyond the short-term risk horizon and incorporate concepts beyond the merely more tangible criteria. It should include variables such as confidence, controllability, interdependence and proximity to try to capture uncertainty and complexity. There are indeed alternatives out there to traditional risk management. A range of tools are available – among them scenario planning (see 'What the literature says about … Scenario Planning') – which are not designed primarily to provide an accurate prediction about a single future but to make you appreciate the variance and richness in predictions. Alertness requires tools and techniques that not only help project managers deal with the repeated past but also allow us to address uncertainty and complexity in our predictions.

WHAT THE LITERATURE SAYS ABOUT …
Scenario Planning

A plethora of literature exists about planning tools and techniques. Much of such literature provides a prescriptive account of what one should do. There appears to be less discourse about the assumptions underpinning these techniques, and therefore about the underlying basis for the planning techniques in use. One promising tool – Scenario Planning – stands out, yet its use has not been widespread and it is not often advocated within the project practitioner literature.

Scenario planning is traditionally a strategic tool which could effectively be used more operationally in project management. While scenario planning has its origins in military strategy studies, it was transformed into a business tool by, among others, Wack [1] and Schoemaker [2]. In contrast to risk management that drives the anticipation of individual risks, scenario planning caters to multiple future realities and encourages thinking in extremes, both possible and plausible.

The aim of scenario planning is the definition of a group of possible and plausible (not necessarily probable) futures that should constructively challenge each other [3–5]. In comparison with traditional risk management, this approach does not aim to focus attention on quantifying a single future; rather, it provides multiple, more abstract projections of alternative futures.

Scenario Planning is a powerful tool if applied in a non-threatening environment. For scenario planning to take effect the culture of an organisation needs to be 'open-minded' with:

1. Receptiveness to multiple, sometimes divergent, perspectives.
2. Openness to having one's views questioned and challenged.
3. The use of a leader or facilitator who can manage the process of scenario planning in a controlled but non-threatening manner.
4. Willingness to provide resources to deal with important issues that may occur.
5. Acknowledgement that scenarios are uncertain in their predictive power and that the 'truth' will not be forthcoming through this technique.

There is much written about scenario planning, so we will provide just a brief overview here of the key stages to work through.

First, identify the drivers for your industry (or project) that are uncertain. Some future trends can be forecast with reasonable accuracy, for example demographics and population growth. Others, though, are far more unclear. These can include, for example, the future oil price (a major issue in determining investment choices in the petroleum industry), anticipated or unknown changes in the regulatory or political environment (upcoming elections create uncertainty and business investment is often delayed until outcomes are known), regional geopolitical uncertainty, future interest rates or the impact of technological innovation.

The next stage is to work out a response for each of these scenarios. For example, if sales are low, we could respond with increased advertising, consider a price change or even a rapid redesign if customer feedback indicates that some aspect should be modified. If sales are high, might we perhaps even need to consider expanded factory capacity? A competitor product introduces different challenges. How close is their alternative to our offering, and how does its performance and price compare? This can lead to a wide range of response options.

Initial brainstorming to identify responses is valuable and allows team members to contribute ideas and opinions. This is not a one-off event, though. Scenarios can be refined and options generated as more data become available. It is therefore a 'living' process as clarity is generated. It can sometimes be useful to have a 'war room' in which data are collated and shared visually and discussions can be had regarding not only the 'what-if' questions, but also to take account of the new and unfolding situation at regular intervals.

Leading the Art of Noticing

Making people 'aware' in a project is a challenge and requires a leadership approach that generates honesty, transparency and openness about risks and uncertainties. We do not suggest a state of paranoia in which a project is constantly thinking and 'living' failure. Such a state may only lead to exhaustion and fatalism. However, a state of 'chronic unease' [6] – a heightened and yet focussed awareness of failure – is one that we can strive for. The following actions may provide a start.

Battling Complacency

The prolonged perception of the absence of failure, good as it might feel, is most often an indicator that people have taken their eye off the ball. At the centre of battle against complacency is the need to make people uncomfortable by challenging them and making them less certain. Certainty about future results is comforting and pleasing, but it can be illusory. Try to play the role of 'Mr/Ms Sceptic'. Be sceptical about people's optimism that everything is going according to plan. With the help of scenarios, cultivate possible outcomes to make people think of what they should be looking out for to prevent these things from happening. Provide them with a safe culture to speak up about whatever concerns them. Even if these concerns are not tangible enough to make it on to a risk register, they are valuable pieces of information that may indicate a creeping crisis. In this sense, worrying is positive and valuable. First and foremost, do not try to battle complacency by turning it into a 'tick-box' exercise. Forms and documents cannot capture subtle but important information such as emotions and gut feelings.

You may pick up signs of complacency. In meetings, people may be preoccupied with sharing their successes. Status reports may outline what has been achieved. It is the task of a leader to acknowledge and celebrate success, but also to put a question mark after every success story and to ensure time is available to raise concerns. Subtly change the way the discussion is going from what has gone right to what might still go wrong.

Moving the Onus of Proof

Our minds like a state of 'normality'. Long periods of success may only reinforce the perception that failure will not trouble us. Managing projects can turn into a routine exercise, and indeed, this is what most managers strive for. Under these conditions, the expectation can become one of continuing success and it may be hard to persuade project participants of contrary possibilities.

The longer this positive state of affairs continues, the more difficult it can become to raise doubts and concerns. Evidence may be ignored or suppressed, with those speaking up seen as doomsayers or troublemakers. Here, managers need to move the onus of proof. Assume that the project is risky, uncertain and complex until proven otherwise. When presented with audits and status reports that show a lot of 'green', show doubt and investigate; challenge people in their perceptions. This does not have to be confrontational but should go below the 'surface' figures to challenge assumptions and create greater awareness of how the project could still go off track.

Many audits in projects provide proof that everything is 'all right' (organisational incentives tend to encourage this). As a thought experiment, can you imagine an audit that provides evidence of risk, uncertainty and complexity and yet also offers also some form of evidence that the project is in a state of heightened preparedness and readiness to deal with it? That is not the kind of audit often used in projects, yet it offers a tantalising glimpse into an entirely different way of understanding project risk and uncertainty.

Making People Imagine

We tend to focus on risks because they are tangible and measurable and thus provide us with the comfort of (relative) certainty but with the help of some tools, such as scenario planning, we can make people imagine uncertainty – ambiguous and difficult to measure – from a range of different perspectives. This is unlikely to provide accurate predictions about how the future will unfold, but it makes people appreciate the richness of multiple possible futures. It also gives 'permission' to worry, express doubts and raise concerns that cannot necessarily be quantified in 'traditional' risk management. The inability to 'prove' a problem must not preclude its being aired and management support for such a culture is powerful (not to mention uncommon). As a project leader, you can – and should – use tools that strive for accuracy and prediction. Know their limitations! Use additional techniques, not for the purpose of determining a single, most likely future, but to strive to explore the murky uncertainties that normally remain undiscussed.

What we cannot measure and articulate with confidence makes us uneasy. It is preferable to stay in our comfort zones, and not worry about, let alone raise, such concerns. As a manager it is important to allow these ideas to surface and be discussed. To reject someone's worries out of hand, or perhaps challenge them for data, sends a clear signal not to try that again. It is a delicate exercise to build greater vigilance – hard to promote, yet easy to discourage. The key is to make the team 'at ease' with feeling uneasy about their project.

Stripping Adversity of its Negative Connotations

The notion of risk and uncertainty as something 'bad' – although inherently natural – can be confronted by a project leader through providing different labels and connotations. Why not call risk a 'design evolution', for example? Regardless of the label, risk and uncertainty are normal and should be treated as such. We cannot wish them away. Detach the existence of risk and uncertainty from any perception of incompetent planning, and frame its management – proactive and reactive – as an opportunity that justifies some form of reward. For example, proactive responses to risks, irrespective of whether they fully work or not, should be highlighted as having prevented a worse state of affairs. Show your appreciation for the action and point out what could have happened if the measures had not been taken. The message of support for pragmatic responses is an important one. Again, if the organisational culture is one of blame and reprisal, then staff closest to the issues are unlikely to respond and this difficult to change.

Focus on the Issue, not the Person Reporting It

The negative connotations of risk and uncertainty may suppress the will of project members to share and report their concerns – the act of reporting might be interpreted as an acknowledgement of incompetence in preventing the failure in the first place. It is the project leader's task to focus discussion on the reported issue, not on the person reporting it. Hence, any discussion about adversity should be impersonal, although the response should have a clear owner. Risk registers, for example, do not need to include the names of people who identified those risks. The focus must be on the message, not the messenger. Appreciation of where the risk came from can be useful, but the individual identifier needs to be encouraged to come forward, not incentivised to keep quiet.

Encouraging the Sharing of Adversity

It takes effort to share identified risks effectively. Provide your project team members with the freedom, space and time to speak up and share their perceptions. This may involve an 'open-door' policy, or a standing agenda item in project meetings. Project members are then more likely to actually share these encounters with risk and uncertainty with others, to allow everybody on the project to appreciate the potential problems. Often such sharing is done by completing a form which is then reflected in an impersonal spreadsheet. Use the power of interpersonal interaction to augment this. By all means use the necessary documentation, but build on it with more socialised sharing. People buy into stories and 'real', personal, accounts of risk and uncertainty far more than into reading a document. Make risk and uncertainty 'alive' to others and encourage people to speak up!

The Impact of Noticing on Relationships

Noticing more – in principle – is a good thing. However, it has the potential drawback that it may confuse and unnerve your stakeholders. You may appreciate the nuances of your project and be comfortable with the discomfort of ambiguity, but it can be challenging to communicate this to your stakeholders.

Certainty is an Illusion

Being on the lookout and noticing an increasing range of risk and uncertainty is a tacit acknowledgement that 'standard' planning concepts are perhaps flawed. All the efforts that have gone into predicting the future, although valuable, are insufficient to completely design risk and uncertainty out of the project. They are still there, and therein lies the opportunity. Projects are often sold on the premise of planning, prediction and control, so stakeholders can sit back and see a plan turn into reality. Stakeholders such as sponsors need to understand that risk and uncertainty is 'normal' and that, despite all the efforts that go into planning, estimates remain estimates. Many aspects remain unknown. Without such an acknowledgement, there is limited need for vigilance and desire to look beyond what has been planned for. Have you got that acknowledgement from your stakeholders?

BEST PRACTICE

This vignette on shortening the planning horizon looks at arguably one of the most hotly-debated and contested aspects of project management. A range of organisations shorten their planning horizons under the umbrella of 'Agile' project management (please see 'What the literature says about … Project Management as a theory'). However, we wish to highlight that this approach could and should be applied in projects characterised by uncertainty, regardless of whether the fundamental approach to managing uncertainty is a (mini-)waterfall approach, or interactive and incremental.

Iterations

At Intel, projects are predominantly run by following the agile philosophy. Part of that philosophy is the definition of iterations. Iterations are single planning and development cycles, ranging from two to six weeks. These cycles are of fixed lengths within a project but can vary across projects:

> In the past you probably would have had to have gone down the route of explaining to them [stakeholders] that we had six-monthly planning and design cycles and so we'd get to it when we do, its brilliant now to be able to say to them ok well we'll take the requirement, we've got a planning session coming up in say three weeks' time, we'll look at it against all of the other priorities that we've got but hopefully we can get that scheduled and then within seven weeks from now you'll be able to get that new piece of functionality scheduled and it is something that our business stakeholders are really appreciating and it just helps to build that partnership with our stakeholders ...

At the end of an iteration there may be the release of an output, the achievement of a milestone, or a design review. However, it is not the output of an iteration that defines its length as duration is fixed for repeatability. Releases to the customer can be made at the end of one or many iterations or more frequently in alignment with customers' needs. After the completion of an iteration, it is reviewed and critiqued by stakeholders – such as the end-user – in order to accommodate flexibility in revising the ultimate goal to be achieved and the way to get there. This form of instrumentalism allows managers to plan an iteration based on learning gained from the previous one:

> You need some certain expectations at the start of a project that the customer has availability and time so they can provide enough input into the project to make sure that we're able to keep the team moving forward at the optimal velocity because if you don't get the feedback then the team kind of stalls ...

The benefits of having such incremental iterations in place are numerous:

- Transparency and visibility: stakeholders receive insight and give feedback not just at the end of a project but throughout.
- Flexibility: frequent reviews and critiques allow timely changes in what to do next and where to go.
- Collaboration: iterations 'enforce' frequent interactions between stakeholders and the provider, with influence from both sides on changing ways of working and the goals to be achieved.

The enablers to achieving such visibility, flexibility and collaboration are based on set expectations. Parties involved need to accept project autonomy, with everyone having their say. That autonomy is built on trust. Iterations are not purposeful if they are only used as a means of checking what another party does.

Instead, beyond providing transparency and thus visibility, they offer a platform to experience progress in delivering a solution while having the comfort of flexibility to change it:

> There's a certain amount of autonomy needed and trust, trust in the customer's point of view, especially if they're maybe funding your particular project, for you to be making decisions ...

> ... you maybe don't want your customer involved in every single one of them but ultimately they will probably affect your output and so having the trust of your customer who in turn then gives you the autonomy to make those decisions on their behalf is an important aspect of it, I think probably that happens to a greater or lesser extent depending on how your project is working, my particular project we take inputs from a variety of different customer groups and stakeholders so we have a number of different masters and we bring those together and try and reconcile all the demand together so we have the autonomy but I think if you're dealing with one particular person, having that ability to make those decisions possibly without the customer's involvement is important.

≡ttpgroup

Another form of using iterative planning is 'Rolling Wave' planning. This is a process whereby you plan part of the project while the work is actually being delivered. As the project proceeds and its latter stages become clearer, additional planning can take place. At the outset, high-level assumptions are made and broad milestones set which become more concrete as the project progresses. As activities are undertaken, assumptions become better defined, milestones become more precise and risks are better understood. Rolling wave planning can be used in circumstances where timescales are particularly tight or where delivery is urgent. In such circumstances, the additional time required for pre-project planning is unacceptable.

At TTP, it is often the case that the client is unsure of exactly what they need to do to solve their problem. Indeed, they may be unsure of the true nature of the problem itself. TTP's project leaders must to be able to adapt their planning:

> ... on say a year's program we have at least three phases in there ... concept phase, detailed design phase and then the transfer to production phase so that at the end of each phase then you can both assess. We can assess and the client can assess – did we achieve the goals? Were we on budget? Is the product within the specification? And all those sorts of things, and so the more phases we have in the better, in some respects, because you're checking it.

Each phase constitutes, in principle, a new contract, yet with shortened planning horizons to allow greater flexibility in adjusting each phase in the light of new information. Rolling wave planning at TTP takes uncertainty into account and provides the benefit of not having to 'fix' the entirety of the project and thus remain inflexible.

The duration of a phase is frequently constrained by functional circumstances. As it is applied in TTP, phases are often defined by their functions of concept, design, and production. Alternatively, phases can be demarcated by a certain level of confidence. The only 'fixed' durations are for those phases for which project managers are sufficiently confident. If estimates are deemed unreliable, the planning horizon will be shortened accordingly. Uncertainty in estimating – characterised by the level of confidence – plays an important role in determining how long a 'wave' may be.

Whether they are called rolling wave or incremental, iterative planning, these concepts have one thing in common – shortening the planning horizon in order to accommodate uncertainty. The flexibility in goals, approach and our interpretation of these aspects – it is all in the eye of the beholder – requires a constant collaboration with all stakeholders involved:

> ... the sponsor will have a lot of influence on it.

At Aviva, similar to what is being prescribed in major agile project management standards, interactions between stakeholders are facilitated in the form of 'Scrum' meetings, for the purpose of opening a discussion on how they could potentially do something differently:

> If someone has a new idea they can feed that back into the scrum so they could say, 'you've asked us to do this to get this result but actually if we did that, you get a better result', and then the project manager would take that back to the business to make sure the new proposal works for them.

Participants at these meetings are all major stakeholders. The meetings do not tend to last longer than 15 minutes, to keep the discussion focussed on relevant reflection and corrections, and also to address the overall project goal and approach.

> We have a daily 15 minutes scrum meeting and everybody that has an interest in this can attend that meeting, including any third party resources that we're using.

For the sake of emphasis, three questions are addressed:

- What did you do yesterday?
- What will you do today?
- Are there any impediments in your way?

These questions may sound mundane and, if repeatedly asked, stakeholders might find them distracting and irrelevant. However the purpose is to ensure the ongoing transparency of what is going on with all the stakeholders together. Issues and blockages can then be quickly resolved, allowing the project to move on.

Traditional project management may entail monthly planning cycles and weekly interactions. However, all our organisations – Intel, TTP, and Aviva – appreciate the need to shorten the planning horizon in their projects; to have short iterations and daily updates.

Reporting Beyond Boundaries

One might assume that the project team does all the noticing and looks out for all risks. But why not enlarge your 'radar' beyond your internal boundaries? Use the wider group of stakeholders as lookouts who are vigilant enough constantly, or at least repeatedly, to raise their concerns with you. Their interests and yours should be aligned with regards to everyone's desire to see the project succeed. If possible, initiate this right at the start of the project, to involve them in predicting risks and imagining beyond a short-term risk horizon. This can create a shared understanding of the project environment and how best to handle it. Without their engagement as part of project radar, they may interpret any unplanned change as a 'surprise'. Their tapped capability to notice and share may be something that needs to be considered when the contract is set up.

You have a choice. You can choose to 'sell' your project by showing (off) your planning and portraying the project as certain. In this case, there may be limited need to be on the lookout for uncertainty, difficult as it may be to do so anyway. However, you also have the opportunity to use your stakeholders' capability to be on the lookout, and consequently to integrate them into your noticing radar. Hence, in meetings with them, feel free to ask about their opinions and gut instincts. Be reluctant to focus solely on what has gone well in a project; drive the discussion about potential failure from a stakeholder's perspective. It is always worthwhile asking 'What do you think might go wrong?'

Consistency in Relationships

The ability to notice and share beyond boundaries forms the pillars of an 'informed' culture, in which all parties understand each other's perspectives, even if they are mutually contradictory. This implies that if stakeholders understand your perspectives, they are more capable of looking out for you and noticing on your behalf. It is less a notion of 'I know better' than a way of adding to the richness of the overall project knowledge and understanding. It requires, however, that you guide your stakeholders to an understanding of your position, and vice versa. Vigilance can only be instilled if parties learn to understand each other's stances through communication, transparency and trust.

Paying for Supposedly Idle Resources

To be vigilant, to notice beyond the measurable and tangible, one needs free time and resources to look out, to challenge others, to encourage and motivate people to do it themselves and actively share their perceptions, perhaps even to think and reflect. Such activities do not necessarily directly contribute to the execution of the project, they 'merely' help you to prepare and ready yourself for something – risk and uncertainty – that may never materialise. Hence, the resourcing of such activities is by no means uncontroversial (especially for budget-holders). A heightened state of awareness comes at price, without necessarily producing tangible and measurable outcomes. Stakeholders require a shared understanding that noticing risk and uncertainty is an art for which faith in its success replaces proof.

WHAT THE LITERATURE SAYS ABOUT ...

Leadership versus Management

Leadership requires a more in-depth insight, as the language of project organising often tends to advocate 'management' and not necessarily 'leadership'. There is a significant difference between these two, and this has been (and still continues to be) the subject of extensive discussion. In his 2009 book *On Becoming a Leader*, Warren Bennis [7, p. 5] gives his understanding of the differences:

- The manager administers; the leader innovates.
- The manager is a copy; the leader is an original.
- The manager maintains; the leader develops.

- The manager focuses on systems and structure; the leader focuses on people.
- The manager relies on control; the leader inspires trust.
- The manager has a short-range view; the leader has a long-range perspective.
- The manager asks how and when; the leader asks what and why.
- The manager has his or her eye always on the bottom line; the leader's eye is on the horizon.
- The manager imitates; the leader originates.
- The manager accepts the status quo; the leader challenges it.
- The manager is the classic good soldier; the leader is his or her own person.
- The manager does things right; the leader does the right thing.

Over the years, a vast body of literature has emerged on the subject of leadership. A number of leadership theories have been developed, and each model has its own assumptions and limitations. There is no 'one size fits all' or 'perfect' leadership solution. Some schools of thought, though, deserve special attention: The *Trait School*, the *Behavioural School*, and the one that is most often cited and referred to, the *Visionary School*.

The Trait School

The *Trait School* had its heyday in the 1940s and 50s. Its view is that leaders are born, not made, with a common set of capabilities. Key traits [e.g. 8, 9] are that leaders are driven and ambitious; they are intelligent, honest and show integrity, are self-confident and also effective problem-solvers.

The Behavioural School

Around the 1960s, the focus was on *behaviours*, the way in which the leader conducts him- or herself [e.g. 10, 11–13]. In principle, this perspective assumes that a leader's behaviour can be conditioned. Some of the parameters include the leader showing concern for people and relationships, including external stakeholders. In addition, behaviours are categorised in terms of styles, such as autocratic, bureaucratic or democratic. It is interesting to note that all of these styles involve sets of behaviours that in principle do not outweigh any other set. Which style is most appropriate is, though, rather context-specific.

The Visionary School

The Visionary school of leadership has probably become the most prominent school since its inception in the 1980s. It encapsulates studies of the success of business leaders. Two fundamentally different types of leadership emerged, *transactional* and *transformational* leadership. MacGregor Burns, [14] Bass, [15] and Bennis and Nanus [16] are a few of the important researchers in this body of knowledge.

Transactional leadership styles tend to focus on maintaining the status quo and ensuring that the smooth operations in place remain that way. This is close to a managerial approach. The 'transactional' terminology refers to the way in which the leader treats subordinates' employment as an exchange of services (labour) for defined remuneration. Extra rewards can be given for exceptional performance, but the motivation mechanisms underlying this tend to be extrinsic. The time horizon for transactional leaders may be shorter and geared towards the here-and-now and the near future rather than where the organisation will be in five, ten or fifteen years from today.

A *transformational leader*, in contrast, has a different view. He or she may be involved less in the day-to-day minutiae of normal operations and will spend more time looking towards the horizon and to where the organisation should be heading. This involves change, new goals and new ways of working, and a vision of an appealing future state. Ideally this should inspire the organisation's members to want to get there, and therefore generate an intrinsic motivation to help on the journey.

These archetypes of transactional leadership and transformational leadership can be thought of as the opposite ends of a continuum. However, they are not mutually exclusive. In practice, leaders will often have to draw on both styles. A purely transformational mode is unlikely to be effective over any extended period of time without a supporting transactional relationship to actually 'get things done' effectively and efficiently.

Such faith in investing in resources that may not make a direct, visible contribution to the delivery of the project can be addressed by distinguishing between value-creating and value-preserving activities. Value-creating activities refer to contributing to the project output. These may include tasks of development and production, and are often emphasised by raising the question of 'What tasks need to be carried out to accomplish the project outputs and outcomes?' Value-preserving activities, such as risk management, are often taken for granted but not really resourced in the same way. Indeed, activities like this that lead towards preventing and containing adversity are often seen as redundant, while value-creating activities are perceived as certain. In budget-constrained times, a culture and an environment in which value-preserving activities are recognised as important are to be welcomed.

Towards an Art of Noticing

The art of noticing is built on the need to look beyond the risk horizon, beyond what we expect to be 'normal'. The benefit is not necessarily to increase the accuracy of prediction, but – to put it simply – to keep on noticing more and become increasingly aware of issues beyond the measurable and familiar. Such a heightened state of awareness can be obtained in a project that is preoccupied with adversity (although without switching to a state of paranoia). Such a project is one in which participants keep their eyes on what might go wrong instead of blindly focusing of what has gone right or is expected to go right.

Reflection

How well do the following statements characterise your project? For each item, select one box only that best reflects your conclusion.

	Fully disagree		Neither agree nor disagree		Fully agree
We acknowledge that our initial estimates are just that, estimates.	1	2	3	4	5
We communicate uncertainty in our planning.	1	2	3	4	5
People are provided with 'space' (e.g. time) to look out for things that could go wrong.	1	2	3	4	5
	Fully disagree		**Neither agree nor disagree**		**Fully agree**
We aim to increase the perceived uncertainty of project participants.	1	2	3	4	5
People are constructively challenged in their estimates.	1	2	3	4	5
We make people think about the things that cannot be specified.	1	2	3	4	5
	Fully disagree		**Neither agree nor disagree**		**Fully agree**
We use intelligent tools and techniques which not only take into account what we know but also what we do not know.	1	2	3	4	5
People are encouraged to share risks and uncertainties, beyond their set boundaries.	1	2	3	4	5
Risk and uncertainty are seen as something 'good' to look out for.	1	2	3	4	5

Scoring: Add the numbers. If you score higher than 27, your capability to notice uncertainty and complexity is good. If you score 27 or lower, please think of how you can expand and enhance your project 'radar'.

References

1. Wack, P., Scenarios: Unchartered Waters Ahead. *Harvard Business Review*, 1985. 63(5): p. 73–89.
2. Schoemaker, P.J.H., Scenario Planning: A Tool for Strategic Thinking. *Sloan Management Review*, 1995. 36(2): p. 25–40.
3. Ralston, B. and I. Wilson, *The Scenario Planning Handbook*. 2006, Mason, Ohio: Thomson Higher Education.
4. Miller, K.D. and H.G. Waller, Scenarios, Real Options and Integrated Risk Management. *Long Range Planning*, 2003. 36(1): p. 93–107.
5. Mulvey, J.M.R., D.P. Rosenbaum and B. Shetty, Strategic Financial Risk Management and Operations Research. *European Journal of Operational Research*, 1997. 97(1): p. 1–16.
6. Reason, J., *The Human Contribution: Unsafe Acts, Accidents and Heroic Recoveries*. 2008, Farnham: Ashgate Publishing.
7. Bennis, W., *On Becoming a Leader*. 2009, New York: Basic Books.
8. Turner, R.J. and R. Muller, The Project Manager's Leadership Style as a Success Factor on Projects: A Literature Review. *Project Management Journal*, 2005. June: p. 49–64.
9. Kirkpatrick, A.A. and E.A. Locke, Leadership Traits Do Matter. *Academy of Management Executive*, 1991. March: p. 44–60.
10. Adair, J., *Effective Leadership: A Self-Development Manual*. 1983, Aldershot: Gower.
11. Blake, R.R. and S.J. Mouton, *The New Managerial Grid*. 1978, Houston: Gulf.
12. Hershey, P. and K.H. Blanchard, *Management of Organizational Behaviour*. 1988, Englewood Cliffs: Prentice Hall.
13. Slevin, D.P., *The Whole Manager*. 1989, New York: Amacom.
14. MacGregor Burns, J., *Leadership*. 2010, New York: Harper & Row.
15. Bass, B.M. and B. Avolio, *The Multifactor Leadership Questionnaire*. 1995, Palo Alto: Mind Garden.
16. Bennis, W. and B. Nanus, *Leaders*. 2003, New York: HarperCollins.

Chapter 4
THE ART OF INTERPRETING

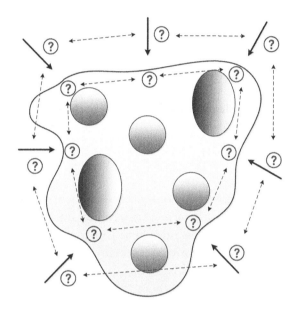

A key factor underpinning the complexity of working in projects is that, although we would like them to be stand-alone entities that we can manage as such, they are actually embedded in a wider ecosystem. Projects are not closed systems but, rather, they are open and necessarily interact with their organisational environment. This significantly adds to the challenge that managers face and even seemingly simple and straightforward projects often belie their complexity. Sometimes the complexity is clearly apparent – perhaps it involves new technologies or innovative methods and processes. However, the complexity often lies in the less apparent, such as a diverse range of stakeholders or changing market conditions.

In these complex projects, risk and uncertainty reside. In part, project planning is used to try to tame some of their effects. This seeks to reduce problems to simple cause-effect relationships and break the messy, complex, problem that is the project into a series of smaller, discrete, parts that can be more readily understood and managed. This not only applies to scheduling and costing, but also to planning for possible risks. However, in doing this, one can lose sight of the 'wider' complexity. In complex sociotechnical systems, cause and effect are rarely straightforward and they can be two-way. If X changes Y, then changes in Y may in turn have a knock-on effect on X. Additionally, simple cause-effect relationships fail to allow for multiple variables and may limit our understanding of systemic underlying causes.

The Lure of Simplicity

The process of simplification is inherently risky. It can encourage complacency and an ignorance of the complexity and the attendant risks and uncertainties associated with that complexity. One can argue that the project team is complicit in a kind of delusion.

Optimism Bias

The project is often understood in terms of its constituent elements, for example using a work breakdown structure. This produces a seemingly (relatively) simple set of tasks and activities and there is a corresponding tendency for the project team to regard the project as being reasonably straightforward. 'Optimism bias' is the term used to describe the tendency to be overly positive about one's ability to achieve something. While a positive attitude is clearly beneficial in a team, this optimism may lead to a failure to reflect reality. People are often unaware that they are being overly optimistic and consequently underestimate the threat of risk and uncertainty. Lateness and overspend may well ensue. The risk planning process may only reinforce this false optimism, because it breaks the risks down into neat categories for which a contingency plan can be developed. It is not unreasonable for project workers to be confident, following a risk planning exercise, that risk has been dealt with.

Normalising

Novelty tends to get absorbed and normalised within processes. With 'normalisation', past experiences become routinely-embedded practices. Risk normalisation (sometime called the normalisation of deviance) involves turning unacceptable behaviours into acceptable behaviours. This happens because people become desensitised to the risks around them – risk becomes 'expected'. The result is that high levels of risk become acceptable at a subconscious level, especially if long periods go by without any undue outcomes from risky situations. For example, working on a building site with no hard-hat may be fine for years. Eventually, however, a negative consequence will surface.

If risk has been normalised, then the emerging risk will catch the project team unprepared, most likely exacerbating the consequences.

'No Effect on Me'

Going hand-in-hand with optimism bias is the belief among many that disaster will not affect their project. They have planned it meticulously and carried out a detailed risk planning and management process. Just as no-one on their wedding day believes that their marriage will end in divorce, so too project workers tend to believe that their project is invulnerable or, perhaps, impervious to risk. They do not think this is without agency – they feel that there is something special about them and what they do that will avert problems, either as individuals or as a collective. The result is that they are likely to focus on 'doing the job' (i.e. working on project tasks) rather than looking for those early, weak signals. Crises and disasters may hit other projects, but they will not happen in this project.

Oversimplification

Because we tend to look at risks and uncertainties in isolation, we often tend to pay little heed to the 'big picture'. Aristotle's famous 'The whole is greater than the sum of its parts' is valid in projects, too. Yet, by applying traditional planning tools, we can emphasise our tendency to oversimplify and thus underestimate risk, uncertainty and complexity. Projects are all about inter-relationships and interdependencies and failure to understand this is to seriously underestimate the risk to project delivery and project outcome.

The Realm of Probability and Impact

Risk management is driven by a relatively simple principle – the likelihood of an event occurring and the probable impact should that event occur. This straightforward approach (likelihood x severity) underpins nearly all standard risk assessments. The orthodox approach is to focus on those risks with a high combination of the two and ignore, or downplay, those with a low probability of occurrence or a low impact should they occur, or both. This can be problematic. How do we know that these measures (estimates) are correct and does this draw attention away from those risks that actually matter more? For example, the result of this analysis might be that we focus on non-critical risk events, or that we ignore wider business or environmental risks that are harder to quantify.

Estimates Become Commitments

The future is difficult to predict accurately and to explain but, at the beginning of projects, this is exactly what a planner is asked to do. Project planners are required to forecast the duration and cost of a project, frequently in the face of intense uncertainty. The estimate they arrive at is essentially the process of putting a value against that uncertainty, governed by a combination of experience and the information available at the time. Owing to the subjective nature of estimating, it can be an inherently personal, human-made, fact-based fiction that we tell ourselves about the time and resource commitment necessary to complete a task. This is a function of not only the project's inherent difficulties, but also our own capacity to combat them. Perhaps the key problem with estimating projects is that the estimate is based on an idealised conception of productivity – an idealisation often based on optimism. The real problem happens when the project team and sponsors equate the estimate with a firm commitment. Estimates are probabilities and commitments cannot be made to probabilities [1]. There is a danger that the commitments to budget and timescale, which are based on the educated guesses made in the estimates, become fixed and immovable, with stakeholders forgetting that they were only estimates in the first place. This can have an unwanted effect on behaviours. Organisations that demand adherence to original estimates unwittingly promote 'padding' in the next set of estimates to increase the likelihood of meeting them. Too much padding – although a perfectly rational response from each individual's perspective – makes the estimate uncompetitive and may lead to the loss of a bid or the work not even being funded.

Anchoring

When estimates have become commitments, these commitments serve as anchors for subsequent decisions about what resources to commit to the project. The tendency to do this is due to over-optimism about the reliability of the estimate. Because of the optimism bias which was built into the original figures, any subsequent analysis is also skewed to over-optimism. Data disconfirming those estimates are discounted and those reinforcing the estimates are amplified. The results are exaggerated benefits, unrealistic costs, and an almost inevitable project disappointment.

Amnesia

People will often try to put difficult or trying times behind them by simply forgetting about them – 'out of sight, out of mind'. Attention moves on to something else (for example, a new project) and people frequently stop thinking about the difficulties they previously faced. Project amnesia is a kind of social amnesia which finds organisations losing memories of past experiences. This can happen simply because people do not want to think about troubling times, or because some staff move on (retire, move to new organisations) and knowledge is dissipated. Having to tackle emerging risks is difficult for project workers. It is no surprise that they, and the organisations they work for, will therefore forget about them over time. It is a well-established phenomenon within the literature that organisations struggle to learn from previous projects. As a result, when risks appear in projects, people often face the challenge of dealing with them as if they were previously unheard of.

The Perception of Losses and Gains

We tend to interpret potential gains and losses differently. Facing a loss triggers stronger stimuli to respond than facing a gain or an opportunity [2]. In a project, a potential loss may thus receive more attention than is given to a possibly more valuable opportunity. Once materialised, actual losses may be a focus for attention while more beneficial opportunities remain under- or unexploited. This response system can create a spiralling effect, where managers stubbornly try to make up for lost ground, missing alternative options that would, when viewed objectively, offer more advantageous uses of time and resources.

WHAT THE LITERATURE SAYS ABOUT ...
Project Complexity

Risk in projects can be thought of in a number of different ways. One approach is to classify risk in terms of its nature and another in terms of its scale [3]. The nature of risk covers aspects such as the familiar technical, physical, environmental and financial sources, but might also include less obvious causes such as the temporal, cultural and social risks associated with the people involved in the project delivery. Maylor et al. [4] identify three different sorts of complexity: 'structural' (such as size, interconnectedness and technical difficulty), 'socio-political' (people, power, politics) and 'emergent' (the occurrence of the dynamic and the unexpected).

Organisations faced with multiple, complex, sources and scales of risk have a variety of approaches in handling them. Approaches such as engineering estimates, probability distributions around net present value and actuarial projections can help to make sense of financial and technical risks. Insurance systems are used for product or service liability [5, 6].

The problem with these approaches is that they are solution-led, focusing on technical and quantifiable risks where an optimal solution can be established through careful and persistent analysis of refined sub-problems. Hancock [7], Holt [8] and Hancock and Holt [3] drew on problem theory to help understand the different ways in which risks manifested themselves in projects and how people might comprehend them. They termed technical, quantifiable risks that were amenable to typical analyses 'tame' risks: these are linear in nature and can be broken down and solved. Where risk management falls short is in tackling more complex risk sources. They used the term 'messy' risks to refer to those risks where the problems were founded in highly complex technical factors. Where the source of the risk was rooted in human behaviour dynamics with multiple stakeholder interests, they used the term 'wicked' risks. Finally, they coined the term 'wicked messes' for those risk sources that were not only technically complex but also socially and behaviourally complex (see Table 4.1).

Table 4.1   Increasingly complex risk [8, p. 261]

	Tame risks	**Messy risks**	**Wicked risks**	**Wicked messes**
Destination	Ends or goals are prescribed or apparent	Ends and means are unknown at the outset, to a lesser or greater degree	End is never fixed, means always invoke qualitative judgements; variable methodologies	End is non-existent; variable world-views. Plausible alternative solutions can always be found
Nature of risk	Analytical or algorithmic solution	Iterative, pan-system and evolutionary	Trial and error; no final strategies; discipline from constant testing	Holistic (structural and mental); revolutionary
Examples	Lexical ordering Analytical geometry	Architecture Epidemic control Lean production Migration patterns	Diversity policy Psychometric testing	Urban design Ecological management
Resolution	Linear, self-referential dialogue	Explorative, non-linear, systems analysis	Explorative, non-linear, disposition analysis	Imaginative, often chaotic and rhetorical

It is not that complex, messy and wicked risks are beyond comprehension. It is simply that they do not lend themselves to clear and unequivocal resolution. They will always involve ambiguity and are never fully determined. This lack of a clear resolution discourages involvement and commitment – what is the point of tackling something where there is no end point? They become side-lined into the realms of uncertainty, away from analysis, with the perception that project teams will work through them should they arise.

Holt [8] notes that where there is dynamic complexity (messy situations) many organisations are alive to the challenges this brings. They are good at redefining boundaries and understanding engineering systems that can encompass broader interrelationships. However, where they tend to be less adept is in tackling behavioural complexity, and where this behavioural complexity is linked to dynamic complexity, it may seem impossible to contemplate the nature of these kinds of risk. If risk of this type is ever tackled, it is generally by recasting the problems as messy or tame risks.

In practical terms, because the nature and methodology of tame risks can be readily understood, the approach adopted is simply to gather data to formulate and implement a solution. With messy risk, the nature of the problem may be understood but the means of tackling it might be more problematic. Here, the chosen approach might be to develop cross-functional teams and undertake systems engineering to resolve the messiness. With wicked risk, neither the nature nor the means of tackling the risk will be fully understood. The best that can be hoped for here is to 'satisfice', focus on priorities and find a way through competing stakeholder needs, wants and world-views (for example, using the MoSCoW method: Must, Should, Could and Would) in order to dissolve the wickedness. Here, problem structuring tools such as soft systems methodologies have been suggested as a means of making sense of the complexity the project team might be faced with [9], while risk leadership, integrating collective knowledge, equitability and conflict resolution are key tenets.

Finding a way through wicked messes is even more difficult. All the approaches that apply to messy and wicked risks would be helpful but Holt [8] adds that psychoanalytic techniques can help both to reveal and expose hidden motives and also to help project workers reconcile themselves to the reality of the complexity they will face.

Key Enablers to the Art of Interpreting

People working on projects tend to underestimate the complexity of the risk and uncertainty they face or, if they can see this complexity, seek to reduce it to simple constituent parts rather than understand and deal with it as a system. What, then, can be done to help people in projects to avoid over-optimism and simplistic thinking?

Interconnections

Perhaps first and foremost, people should be helped to understand the interdependencies between different parts of the project, between the project and the wider environment and between the different stakeholders. While not ignoring the relatively straightforward tame risks, they need to be helped to make sense of the messy and wicked risks and to cope with the wicked messes. At the same time, project workers should be careful not to oversimplify, and to be realistic in terms of their optimism. There are a number of strategies that can be used to help project teams think in terms of connections and relationships. For example, liberal use of 'rich pictures' associated with soft systems methodology (SSM) [10], can help people understand the interconnectedness of project systems. SSM focuses on seeing project systems as mental models of interconnection and is a good way of revealing and understanding different world-views. Understanding connections between elements of a system and across different systems is the first step in avoiding oversimplification and over-optimism. It illustrates, in a very vivid manner, the complexities of projects and the scope for risk to emerge.

BEST PRACTICE

AVIVA

Risk Interdependencies

Many project workers are engaged in multiple projects and switch from one context to another. In doing so, they invariably encounter a common problem for such workers, which is how to make rapid sense of the project environment in which they find themselves and identify ways to apply their knowledge and capabilities quickly and effectively. One project manager told us that project management is often advocated as a mechanism to break down a complex environment into single entities of change which can be managed in isolation of each other. For example, risk management suggests identifying individual risks to which one can respond. Risk management requires a project leader to contain risks before they materialise but this strips out the context of interdependencies and how risks influence each other:

> ... if we take those problems, pull them all together and say, right as a result of doing this we've created this massive problem ...

At Aviva, the issue of interdependencies between risks is actively addressed. In doing so, Aviva is seeking to acknowledge that one risk may influence other risks, not only within the boundaries of a single project but, possibly, also across project and organisational boundaries.

A range of tools is utilised to encourage project leaders to think about risk interdependencies. One tool that can easily be applied to address risk complexity is causal mapping. Causal mapping has its origin in strategic management, but can be applied in any context that involves some complexity (e.g. [11]). At Aviva, this involves visualising interdependencies which are then mapped, often in the form of a cognitive map or mind map (see Figure 4.1).

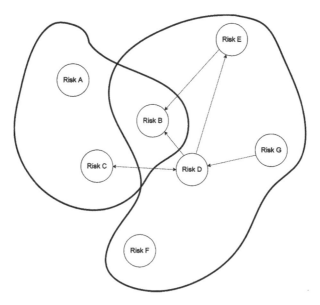

Figure 4.1   Example of a causal map

In this example, particular attention has to be paid to Risk D, as it influences other risks beyond the project boundary.

There is no single right answer as to how to develop these causal maps. Elements can be coloured differently, for example to highlight risks that affect critical components in one or more projects. A key objective of such maps however, is to trigger exploration of problems – risks in this example – but also solutions. As much as risks can interact with each other, so can solutions.

Aviva sees both uncertainty and complexity as issues to be addressed through understanding the interrelationships and seeking practical solutions. It is, of course, a challenge to make objective sense of complexity. To some, it may seem a futile exercise to move beyond the isolationist management of risk to explore risk and response interdependencies. For others, it is a revelation which provides another step in appreciating uncertainty as well as complexity in modern day project management.

Devil's Advocate

There is a misconception about seeking consensus and direction in decision-making through people's engagement in dialogue. This is generally not the best approach if decisions need to be made not only quickly but also effectively. Dialogue involves conversations between people with mutual concerns but no task-orientation or any necessity to persuade others to accept a position. What is more useful in decision-making, where task and direction are important, is dialectics. Dialectics privilege rationality in an argument in order to arrive at a consensual 'truth'. Where groupthink might prevail, the role of the 'devil's advocate' is powerful in arguing against that prevailing position. That role is to resist and to point out flaws, risks and alternatives. The devil's advocate increases both the number and quality of decision-making alternatives and can be a catalyst for new ideas [12]. Devil's advocacy can be used both in early decision-making stages and also as a post-decision critique. It is normally best undertaken by someone separate from the group – an outsider who is both structurally and emotionally detached from the project or problem being considered.

Memory

For projects, organisational amnesia means that past risks, and their causes, can easily be forgotten. A way of tackling this phenomenon is to refresh the memory and surface previous, possibly unpleasant or difficult, experiences. Although a wide range of IT-based codification systems have been developed, it is important to recognise the importance of relationship-based memory within the organisation [13]. Although it is widely studied in the academic literature, the value of social interaction is often underplayed within practitioner-focused work. 'Social capital' (which is comparable to financial or human capital) is often vital in 'getting things done', and most managers intuitively recognise this. Because it is a somewhat intangible concept and hard to quantify, though, organisations are generally reluctant to try and 'manage' it. However, strong relationships build trust and a network of trusted colleagues built over time is hugely valuable. Speaking to someone and using their knowledge often also seems more 'real' and relevant, and even more trustworthy, than reading documents in a lessons-learnt database. In a team-based environment, members also soon learn 'who-knows-what', and this in turn leads to efficiency in knowledge-sharing and knowledge generation that surpasses what would be the case in a newly-formed team.

In order to encourage these activities, some practical things organisations can do are to put in place mechanisms for reflecting and learning from experience; to focus feedback from peers or managers on experiential learning and to support learning both within the team and from outside the team through the sharing of experiences. Some mechanisms that can be put in place to support this kind of learning and prompting of memories are communities of practice and the use of storytelling techniques. The latter are often rich and provoking and have been found to be a very effective way of learning and fixing experiences in the mind [14].

BEST PRACTICE

Maintaining and Retaining Knowledge

Working in a complex environment, it is important to understand what the significant knowledge is (the 'how' of the work), and who the best people are to go to for expertise and advice. Ensuring that this is effective, and that staff can learn from such experts, is a key part of practical knowledge management. As one project manager told us:

> ... especially in the very deep knowledge areas where there's a hugely complex environment, we try and keep knowledge experts in their positions so they can help kind of coach and bring up other people within the team, certainly in some of the projects that we've been involved in where we have almost a core nucleus of permanent employees who are working on a particular project and have done in that particular area for quite some time, you find that the benefits really start to get shared across the team because, if you've got on the periphery of the project, people that are maybe coming and going or aren't around for so long can really learn and be coached by those other people. In the particular area that we work in, where there's a real need for some fairly deep and narrow skill sets, that knowledge is particularly important. You would probably find that if you kept disbanding [the team], although there might be some fairly fundamental technology knowledge and skills that you would be able to transfer, you would lose the broader domain knowledge and the knowledge area, and you would probably see that your velocity or the productivity of the team would suffer as a result.

At Intel, despite the inherent uncertainty in the problems, solutions and stakeholders they are engaged with, they try to maintain pools of project teams so that knowledge and capabilities are as stable as possible. They will add knowledge if required. Technical expertise as well as familiarity are brought together and maintained:

> *... it could be that on one side you have people that are dealing with business intelligence systems and then maybe on the other side you have people that are dealing with customer relationship systems. But if they're all dealing with the same business unit or the same division, that inherent knowledge about how that business unit functions and operates, and even simple stuff like the terminology that people are using, means they know what you're talking about. So, if you are going through in an agile manner, when you're having reviews with customers or you're speaking to your project owner, everyone can use that common language and you don't have to spend half the meeting explaining the ecosystem of that particular business group. Then you can back that up with the technical skills if necessary, down to the level of different databases involved or the different kinds of backend infrastructure systems that are involved. That comes together as a kind of core nucleus of education in that area.*

This 'pooling' of knowledge, however, does not guarantee a commitment to retain it over time. With increasing experience, valuable knowledge workers may be promoted away from where their knowledge is most valuable. Promotion of skilled and knowledgeable staff can deprive projects of expertise. To deal with this problem, Intel developed a culture that encourages experts to remain close and committed to the project at hand. As we were told:

> *It's one of the very strong corporation cultures that we have in terms of making sure that your career develops well. Intel is an organisation that doesn't allow people to get into a 'comfy seat'. We encourage you to continually push you on. Our internal structures allow that, so at every stage they then push you on and you get a greater level of responsibility. Thus, in our project, where we have this core nucleus who have probably been in that kind of role for a while, we start to ask them to start coaching, mentoring the more junior, less experienced, members of the team so that they are almost creating their own succession plan. Then, when it does get to that point where they've reached the level to move up, you've then built up some people behind them that can take over from them. Then, in theory, everything goes smoothly. It doesn't always happen that way of course, and you do sometimes find that you've got a single point of dependency where if they move on you have a hole and you have to scrabble around a little bit more – that takes a bit to manage and you have to make sure that your transition plan is good there. We have this culture where if somebody does move on and you still continue to need their help, we have mechanisms that allow you to contact that person and use some of their time to be able to look back at the old area. It means we can fill some of that gap if one was formed.*

To retain knowledge, one could simply offer a monetary incentive. That is not necessarily the best route, though, since if I am paid more for my specific expertise, I have a strong disincentive to share what I know. This can reward entirely the wrong behaviours. Looking more broadly, knowledge experts...:

- tend to be specialised, yet have an interest in looking beyond their specialism. Employers may offer, in the form of a rotation, insights and challenges from different perspectives.

- tend to believe in independency and often do not like to be 'boxed in' by hierarchy. It is not the hierarchical position that defines a knowledge expert but the value they can offer. The meaning in their work is not really defined by status *per se* but by the development of knowledge that can be accessed for the good of the project. The respect of peers is a strong motivator.
- tend to be lifelong learners. They constantly need to maintain their interest by being challenged and pushing their boundaries. Allowing them to do this and offering them these opportunities keeps them interested, and thus committed and more likely to stay with the organisation.

At Intel, the focus is beyond the mere execution of a project. People in this project are seen as valuable resources, who need freedom and help to pursue their own objectives. This is vital in order to maintain their interest and ensure their commitment in an ever-changing environment.

Value Driven Risk Management

The reason projects are undertaken is to deliver value for the organisation (whether private-, public- or third-sector). This may involve specific products or services and can even encompass safety and regulatory compliance projects. The value in performing the latter can be expressed by considering the business risk and impact of *not* undertaking them. Given (broadly) that business or taxpayer value is the reason for doing projects, it makes sense that there is a focus on value-driven delivery. The concept of risk is closely related to value, so much so that sometimes we think of risk as 'anti-value'. This is because, if they occur, risks have the potential to erode value. The notion of value is also closely tied to differing definitions of success, with project delivery criteria in terms of budget and time frequently overlapping only briefly with the actual business needs of the sponsoring organisation. So following a project plan to conclusion may not in fact lead to success if value-adding changes are not implemented effectively [15].

The purpose of value-driven project management is to shift the focus from the detailed delivery of project activities to understanding what value means for customer and end-user stakeholders and, in doing so, concentrating on what really matters in the project. If this shift happens, then risk management is similarly shifted to concentrate on what is important in terms of project value. This may, for example, mean allowing the timescales or budget to slip if that leads to improved value for the end-user. If the project team is concentrating on this value, then their focus is on the risks that matter and, as a consequence, they give greater attention to some risks over others. It does not mean that risks outside what has been defined as of value are unimportant – they might still have the potential to derail the project – but it should mean that attention is prioritised effectively.

There are a number of techniques associated with this kind of value approach that can be employed. Many have the added advantage of emphasising the creative potential of the project team. Techniques which might be employed to enhance project value include:

- Functional Analysis (sometime called the 'functional analysis systems technique' – FAST). This is a method of analysis that can be applied to the individual functional parts of a project, identifying and emphasising the intended outcomes of the project as opposed to outputs or methods of delivery. Each aspect can be described with a 'verb – noun – phrase or adjective' combination which focuses the thinking.
- Life-cycle costing and whole-life value techniques. Here, the focus is on how costs are incurred and value derived from the outputs of a project right through its useful life. Costs that might be considered include: the original development costs, plus the deployment costs over its lifetime (the total running costs including maintenance and repairs) and any decommissioning costs. In some industries, such as the oil industry and civil engineering, sophisticated modelling is used to establish whole-life value although, even here, the approach founders on how value can be defined.
- Job plan and creativity techniques. Using brainstorming approaches, frequently in multi-disciplinary groups, means that many new ideas can be generated quite simply by asking clear questions. Asking 'How can we do this better/faster/cheaper?' or 'How can we apply what we know to a new product or market?' can generate hugely valuable answers in a short period of time. There is rarely a single, simple, solution to such problems and these approaches are particularly effective in encouraging creativity in the project team.

Leading the Art of Interpreting

Over-optimistic forecasts of likely project performance, based on under-estimating the complexity of projects and the reality of likely risks, coupled with an over-optimistic assessment of the project team's ability to deal with risk and uncertainty, are major problems for project decision-making. As we have seen, estimates have a tendency to become commitments that, in turn, become anchors for later decisions. Given this, projects can become brittle and fragile – the slightest risk might derail them if the original commitments were dangerously optimistic. With very narrow measures of success for the immediate outputs (time, cost, quality), risk occurrences may lead swiftly to failure – that is almost an inevitability. Worse still, people are cognitively hardwired to be optimistic, either for political reasons (getting the project funded or awarded in the first place) or (more often, perhaps) psychologically. We delude ourselves and we are all complicit with each other in that delusion.

The problem faced by project leaders is that they have to find ways of countering this tendency – of stepping back, looking at the project plan with more realistic, dispassionate eyes and injecting some reality (perhaps even pessimism) into the planning process. Project managers are often unable to do this as they are too involved in the 'process' and are as subject to the same cognitive biases as everyone else involved in the work. Instead, the project manager must take a leadership role, focusing on people rather than structure and process, taking a longer-term rather than shorter-term view, challenging the status quo and being innovative rather than administrative. Beyond the practical things that can be done to help balance out optimism bias and organisational amnesia, the project manager *as a leader* has a key role in shaping the forecasts and avoiding over-simplification of the risk and uncertainty involved in delivering the project.

Asking Inconvenient Questions

If the project leader is able to emotionally and structurally detach him- or herself from the project – a difficult enough task – he or she can (as required) slip into the role of devil's advocate that all projects require to combat our tendency to oversimplify. They will be able to challenge the 'inside view' and access an 'outside view' that may be more realistic. They will be able to prompt memory, encouraging the experts to recall past projects and consider what may go wrong, why it may go wrong and how they could deal with any risk and uncertainty. The focus of questioning is to probe limitations in everybody's preparation and readiness and not to question anyone's competence. As inconvenient as these questions may be, they are essential in challenging oversimplification and in encouraging new ways of thinking.

Focussing on Opportunities

A bias towards the negative side – adversity – in a project may focus people predominantly on managing it, so that they largely ignore the potential upside in the form of opportunities. A project leader can try and draw attention to how the team could deliver project outputs and outcomes faster, better and/or cheaper. This is only valid in projects in which deliverables are not set in stone but have incentives for stakeholders to explore and exploit opportunities. It is always valuable to ask the 'Why don't we?' questions.

Distinguishing between Noise and 'Real' Risk and Uncertainty

In adopting a dialectic decision-making role, the project leader can encourage a focus on the important risks, where management attention needs to be focused. The issue is to distinguish between what 'matters' and what does not. Based on an active reporting culture, you may be bombarded with stakeholders' concerns and flooded with 'what might go wrong' in the project. It is the job of a project leader to filter out those important messages that it is vital to respond to. In order not to discourage any report of impending failure, consider all messages as important, though. With the help of the messenger, raise some important questions such as:

- Has this happened before? Is it an indication of systemic risk and uncertainty?
- Might it influence a part/function of the project that is critical?
- How close have you been to this risk/uncertainty? Do we require more information?
- How quickly could this cascade into a bigger threat?

These kinds of questions can enable effective decisions to be made about risk. You can filter out the less important risks and concentrate on those that will impact on value. Be sensitive, though, to the idea that the messenger, as well as the wider team, may be conditioned by optimism bias.

BEST PRACTICE

AVIVA

Project Management Software

Project Management Software can facilitate the activity of scheduling and estimation. It helps to cope with the abundance of information. Aviva uses commercially-available project and portfolio management software as a tool to provide critical information in real time. This system standardises, manages and captures the execution of project and operational activities and resources. It comprises several modules and components to allow the management of project finances, time recording and resources, including demand, risks and issues.

By using one system to manage multiple functions, the project manager can keep all essential information in a single location that is also available to other team members and is therefore easy to keep up to date:

> *I have actually found it quite useful – having all the information in one place and accessible is a real bonus for project managers.*

However, accessing information is not the only benefit a software tool should provide. It should also provide the following:

- Memory: it should be a reminder of the risks, uncertainties and complexities. For example, the system probes the project's commitment to interpret risk and uncertainty and refreshes participants' ability to do so:

  > *So if you do not review your risks by that date, a report pops up to remind you that you need to review this risk. If you leave it too long the governance team will pick you up on it and say "You are not managing your risk and that will get reported up to your manager." It's a great incentive to manage risks well and in a timely manner as no-one wants to be seen to be behind.*

- Simplicity: allowing the 'simplification' of data (but be aware of the danger of oversimplification) to aid decision making.
- Nuanced Appreciation: it should allow one to distinguish between 'hygiene' factors and novel adversity. Hence, it should help identify patterns across projects and flag up any uncertainty.
- Communication: facilitating instant communication. Time stamps highlight how up-to-date the information is.
- Confidence: providing evidence of the validity of information. It should help a project to probe aspects that are unknown.
- Challenge: it should not replace the project leader's role in asking inconvenient questions but should help to tackle people's optimism bias.

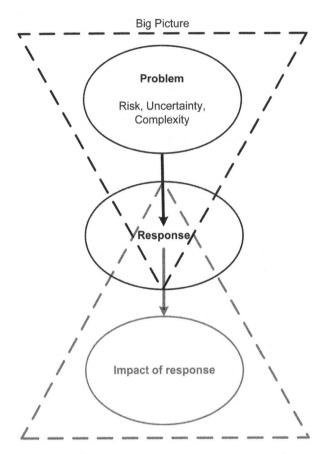

Figure 4.2   Big picture thinking – problem

Addressing the 'So What?' Question

A project leader's responsibility is not only to challenge people on their perceived degree of certainty, but also to create a desire in them to be on the lookout for problems, report the possibility of failure and share their perceptions with other members of the project team. In other words, they need to be alert. Alertness, however, requires addressing the 'So What?' question (see Figure 4.2), beyond the boundaries of project tasks. What do risks and uncertainties mean for a task, a project, the programme and ultimately the business of the key stakeholders? By raising these questions, a project leader increases the project sensitivity beyond their immediate responsibilities, enabling and requiring them to see beyond the short-term demands of project delivery and keep in mind what defines value in the project. This is a critical, driving, focus that demands a desire to keep alert about any change. It is central to retain the perspective of the Big Picture.

Extending the Half-life of Risk and Uncertainty

Where organisational amnesia is present, the experience of risk and uncertainty may quickly fade. This fading can be thought of as the half-life of project learning, with the leader beholden to extend the memory for as long as possible. In the prolonged absence of failure, and with changes in personnel, this half-life can be remarkably short. The project leader's role in this situation is to employ approaches to prompt memory and retain focus on the possibility of failure, particularly where success has been the norm for a protracted period. It is important to remind people of previous risks that have been responded to – what happened and why. Refreshing people's memory of past risk and continuously revising risks and uncertainties might seem arduous and detract from the 'actual' work but, without it, patterns of response may be lost over time.

Regularly reviewing previous risks and the effectiveness of responses to them is a powerful way to facilitate discussion that keeps risk 'alive' in participants' minds and fosters a continual, healthy, scepticism about present project delivery.

Being Optimistic in the Face of the Abyss

It is, of course, important that the project leader stresses the potentially imminent nature of risk and uncertainty arising as a consequence of the complex project environment and the corresponding challenge of identifying what constitutes value in such a context. It is also important that project workers are encouraged to recall and confront the reality of past project experiences so that they do not begin to over-simplify the nature of risk or to normalise risky situations. Additionally, the project leader must play devil's advocate to inject a dose of reality in order to counter over-optimism and curb excessive enthusiasm. Although all this is important if risk is to be meaningfully understood and interpreted within projects, it also poses the danger that the project team may become disheartened and demoralised by a continual preoccupation with failure. They may feel disempowered in the face of seemingly insurmountable complexity where there are no clear resolutions, only half-solutions that satisfy no one. There is a further danger that they may feel nothing they can do will ever allow them to overcome the ever-present risk and that all their planning and risk assessment is pointless. Therefore, another role of the project leader is to guard against a sense of impending fatalism and ennui. The team must be reminded that they are being given capabilities for resilience. The project leader should focus their attention on the long-term outcomes of the project and the benefits it will bring the business, customer, end-users or community.

WHAT THE LITERATURE SAYS ABOUT ...

Optimism Bias

Many studies have shown that project forecasts are notoriously inaccurate [16, 17]. This problem appears to be widespread, with a range of infrastructure and IT projects subject to the phenomenon [18, 19]. Reasons for this seem to centre around over-optimism. Simply put, project planners, managers, owners and others are regularly over-optimistic in their forecasts as to when their projects will be delivered, what they will eventually cost, and what the final performance will be [e.g. 20, 21, 22]. In their research on this topic, Flyvbjerg et al. [20, p. 286] have been forthright in observations of this persistent trend:

> No learning seems to take place in this important and highly costly sector of private decision making. This seems strange and invites speculation that the persistent existence over time, location, and project type of significant and widespread cost under-estimation is a sign that an equilibrium has been reached: Strong incentives and weak dis-incentives for under-estimation may have taught project promoters what there is to learn, namely that cost under-estimation pays off.

Optimism has a number of impacts, including reducing pressure on the project team to be productive [23], and allowing organisations to out-compete competitors to win project awards [24, 25]. Research has provided a number of explanations for optimism bias [26, 27], which can be categorised as technical, political and psychological.

Technical

'Technical error' encompasses unreliable or inaccurate data, the absence of data or the use of imperfect forecasting techniques [e.g. 28]. De Meyer, Loch and Pich [29], in their comparison of new product development projects, identified four sources of technical error when making forecasts (see also [22, p. 1072]):

1. The level of variation (the difference between this project and previous ones).
2. 'Foreseen uncertainty' (the level of predictable emergence during the project).
3. 'Unforeseen uncertainty' (the level of unpredictable and unplanned-for emergence during the work).
4. The level of chaos (the unpredictability in the initial and underlying conditions and the unforeseen nature of the final outcome).

In a complex world, it is impossible to predict accurately the future state of the project and its environment. Consequently, technical errors and, therefore, over and under-estimation in project forecasts will always occur. However, empirical testing has found that technical explanations for optimism bias may be discounted. Technical explanations would suggest a normal distribution of over- and under-optimism over time but, instead, there is evidence of a significant tendency towards optimistic forecasts, suggesting that political and/or psychological explanations are more useful [30].

Political

Some researchers have observed signs that deliberate under-estimation of costs and over-estimation of the benefits and the speed of the work are common in order to gain approval and funding for the project [20, 31]. Frequently, this form of 'deception' is used by project teams and managers in order to increase the likelihood of getting their projects funded [32], with overpromises of what they can achieve just to get it started. Frequently, budgets are unrealistically small and the bidding process encourages over-promising. Additionally, because funders frequently want to have use of project outputs as quickly as possible, time is generally insufficient for close scrutiny of bids, project plans and promises [33]. Indeed, Flyvberg has gone as far as to suggest that other stakeholders, including funders, can be complicit in this deception in an effort to ensure that projects are initiated [30].

Psychological

This political 'deception' within project forecasts is an intentional (and common) behavioural strategy, generally aimed at increasing the bargaining leverage for funding and acceptance. However, human judgement may be influenced by an unconscious desire to inject optimism bias into project forecasts. Yates [34] carried out detailed studies showing optimism bias as a result of over-confidence in human judgement. People appear to share a tendency towards planning bias, leading to over-estimated project scope and under-estimated completion and cost estimates, a tendency that may, in part, be responsible for poor outcomes for many private and public projects in the UK [e.g. 18, 35, 36].

Lovallo and Kahneman [37], in their ground-breaking research, noted that when they were thinking of the future, individuals generally had an overly positive view of themselves, and rated likely outcomes more positively than those of other people. Known as the 'planning fallacy', individuals were seen to hold more confident and optimistic predictions because they believed more strongly in their own talents and the impact they would have over their environments (known as the 'inside view'), while they de-emphasised evidence of their inability to be so effective in similar tasks in the past (the 'outside view'). In the case of decision-makers faced with the need to act, this dissociation of the past from the present is magnified. This wishful thinking and the illusion of control lead to doubts about decisions being suppressed [38, 39]. This is exacerbated by the desire to give people the answers they want to hear and to give an impression of a safe and predictable world [40]. In addition, people tend to hold a number of self-deceptions which lead to an overall optimism bias [41], a phenomenon that has been described as unrealistic optimism [42] or comparative optimism [43]. There are five factors leading to unrealistic optimism [22, p. 1073]:

1. People's predictions tend to mirror their hopes and ambitions for desired outcomes. Rather than considering past outcomes, wishful thinking is applied and current intentions are projected into desirable outcomes of future events.

2. Rooted in attribution theory, past successes tend to be attributed to internal causes such as personal ability and resilience, while failures are attributed to external forces, such as unfortunate circumstances or a particularly difficult task [44]. This is important because explanations of why successes or failures occurred have an important effect on whether information about a past event will be considered important in predicting the outcome of a future event.

3. Individuals tend to overestimate their personal role in positive outcomes related to events of the past – what is also known as the egocentricity bias [45].

4. Although individuals who are high in dispositional optimism are better at identifying suitable goals and tend to have confidence in achieving them, when they are not able to identify an attainable goal there is a tendency to stay committed to the unattainable goal or disengage from goal attainment [46].

5. People go through two basic cognitive mechanisms in order to form expectations [47]. During the first stage a search for evidence is undertaken, favouring knowledge which is consistent with the desired outcome and thereby reinforcing optimism bias. In the second stage of formation expectation, selected evidence is evaluated. At this point in the process, information undergoes differential scrutiny, once again leading to bias.

It seems, then, that optimism bias is a very common and very normal human trait. In part, this can be attributed to lack of available information and to political manoeuvring but largely, optimism seems to be cognitively hardwired into people. This has profound implications for decisions made at the early stages of projects, where commitments are made to deliver within timescales and resource budgets and where risk is being considered.

Allowing People to Appreciate Different Perspectives

Perhaps one of the biggest early challenges for a project is to find a means of including and capturing the perspectives of multiple stakeholders. This is, of course, entirely dependent on the precise nature of the project being undertaken but stakeholders rarely speak with one voice, even where they might represent a single organisation. For example, it has been observed that for large, general, hospitals, each department (e.g. A&E, cardiology, diagnostic imaging, gastroenterology, maternity, obstetrics and gynaecology, radiotherapy, etc.

and even the chaplaincy and pharmacy) will have competing demands, needs and wants from the project. How is the project team to capture and balance the different views of these multiple stakeholders? This is before patient groups, ancillary staff and other interested stakeholders have been considered. The project team may well find that these perspectives can be at odds with each other, which risks damaging the project. This is why value-driven project risk management is so important in such a situation. The project leader's role here is to provide the space and opportunity to make sense of the multiple perspectives at play and understand them as a source of risk and uncertainty.

Be careful, though. It is not sufficient to approach these potentially divergent opinions with a view to averaging and normalising them. If we just reduce the richness of different perspectives to a single estimate, we may oversimplify. The richness of different perspectives may be captured and used to understand better the nuances of the project so that pragmatic and context-specific solutions can be crafted and shared.

The Impact of Interpreting on Relationships

A large number of people have only a limited appetite for risk and uncertainty. This is not necessarily good news for our project. Stakeholders such as funders, sponsors and end-users all crave certainty and simplicity. They want to realise the benefits as soon as possible with a clearly set out investment of resources. However, most real-world projects are, to some extent, complex and they inherently contain risk and uncertainty. It is incumbent on the project team and, in particular, the project manager/leader, not only to demonstrate competence in understanding and being prepared for this but also to disabuse stakeholders of the notion that any project is without such risks. It is through this understanding that they will be more able to focus on and draw value from the project. It can be a difficult message to convey, and individuals may not wish to hear it but, if the stakeholders are to avoid delusions of success [43], it is in their collective interests to engage with this message.

Be Reluctant to Commit to Singularity

Be aware of estimates turning into commitments. If we think about single estimates, we expect them to happen. As a project leader, it is important that uncertainty in estimates is highlighted through signposting and labelling. For example, an estimate can be given with a corresponding confidence level, and/ or the use of upper and lower bounds. It is also down to the language that is used to express uncertainty in our predictions. The simple use of 'may' and 'might' provides a necessary – although inconvenient – signpost to stakeholders that project planning is still a look into an unknown future.

A good example of careful, planned management of the message of the estimate was the London 2012 Olympics. Initially starting off at £2.4 billion when the Games were awarded to London, over the succeeding years, this was increased to a final budget of £9.3 billion. The fact that the budget was going to increase over time was clearly conveyed to the Government and public at large and, when the final costs were calculated, the media reported that the Games had actually come in under budget.

Whether the project team are doing a single point estimate or a range bound estimate, it is important to note that they are still just estimates. They should not be confused with commitments or constraints and they should be used with that in mind. Unless this distinction is clear, the results could be painful. This however, does not mean that estimators can throw caution to the wind and produce completely unreliable numbers. Things to look out for when reporting estimates to a wider stakeholder community are:

- Padded estimates – it is tempting to pad and buffer estimates through building in contingencies and assumptions. Sometimes, this is an appropriate procedure but in general it is to be avoided. All it really does is create distrust in the overall reliability of the estimates which are, in turn, compromised.
- Failing to revisit estimates – just as the project team should revisit and reassess risk analyses, so too they should continually revisit and reassess estimates. As more information becomes available, so the assumptions and contingencies built into the estimate become easier to assign.
- Avoid taking estimates at their face value – sometimes teams are either over-confident or unduly pessimistic with their forecasts. It is one of the jobs of the project leader to find ways of validating and reconciling these estimates before using them as a source for planning or any other decision-making. This is where the role of the devil's advocate is important, particularly in tandem with a focus on value.
- Avoid ignoring task dependencies – projects are rarely considered as systems with tasks and activities that have complex interrelationships both within the project and with external systems. These interdependencies introduce risk and uncertainty.

- Communication of estimates – a great deal is at stake in the communication of the estimates. They require the buy-in of influential stakeholders but must also be communicated in such a way that they do not encourage a false certainty.
- Avoid 'guesstimates' – estimates that are not based on historical project data, industry standards, reasonably detailed analysis or any other generally accepted method are not estimates, they are just guesses.
- Analysis is important – the first step in ensuring a resilient project is to seek to analyse the project environment as accurately as possible, including as many risks as can sensibly be incorporated. The risk analysis should be captured in the estimate and tracked and updated regularly.
- Be wary of silos – estimating is not a single person's responsibility, although one individual may be responsible for consolidating and communicating the estimates. Estimating is improved by getting consensus and broader understanding, and the more involved the team members are in gathering and discussing the estimates, the more accurate the results are likely to be.

Selling Capabilities to Deal with Uncertainty, not the Illusion of Certainty

Project experts are often held up as paragons of planning who are able to bring control to what might otherwise be chaos. They come armed with a plethora of techniques and processes that set them apart from other managers and it is these capabilities that form the basis of the relationship between the project team and key sponsors and other stakeholders. The idea is to instil confidence in stakeholders that this team will succeed through careful preparation. Perhaps understandably, given the desire for certainty and simplicity, this tends to downplay the role of risk and uncertainty in projects. However, it gives a false impression that the risk and complexity of projects is somehow 'tameable' and can be significantly reduced, or even eradicated. Rather than starting out on this footing, it might be more useful to form relationships with the stakeholders that acknowledge that complexity and risk are ever-present, and that the real capability of the project team is to deal with this situation. In part this is done through careful planning and control, but it also draws on the capabilities of resilience. A chief part of this resilience is the ability to understand and make sense of risk in context.

Understanding the Diversity of Perspectives ... Repeatedly

Behavioural and cultural complexities are pervasive in projects. Multiple stakeholders bring with them multiple perspectives of what the project means to them and, moreover, these perspectives are liable to change as the project progresses. As we have seen, this is a 'wicked' source of risk, which can arise even in projects that are otherwise relatively technically straightforward.

Value-driven project risk management offers a number of techniques which can be used to find and make sense of the value that stakeholders wish to derive from the project. However, this cannot be just a one-off exercise, undertaken at the beginning of a project to allow it to proceed. Just as perspectives of value are relational, contextual and dynamic, so are the attendant risks and uncertainties. If the project team is seeking to understand and meaningfully interpret risk in the project, it needs to be continually attending to the multiple perspectives stakeholders will bring. In this way, it can track and grasp the changing nature of risk and uncertainty as it unfolds through the life of the work.

Towards an Art of Interpreting

The realistic interpretation of risks and uncertainties is constrained by our longing for simplicity. We often break down a complex environment into its parts and look at them in isolation. Such thinking is amplified by our tendency to underestimate the impact of each risk and uncertainty. There is help, though. Our desire to make sense of the future through simplification should not be replaced altogether, but it should be challenged. Being a devil's advocate and raising a series of inconvenient questions may start us on a journey to the appreciation and embracing of uncertainty rather than to ignoring it.

BEST PRACTICE

≡ttpgroup

Organisational Identification and Belonging

How individuals determine value for themselves is a deciding factor in choosing to join an organisation or project. The extent to which members commit to something as temporary as a project is very much dependent on the value of belonging and on identifying one's values with those of the project and the organisation. The sense of belonging at TTP is driven by the creation of personal relationships. It is:

> ... one of the most powerful things. People will join resources from the other groups and they make a personal bond.

After-work social groups, sports teams and working on community issues all help foster a sense of shared purpose including,

> ... the fact that they eat in the same restaurant, that sort of social mixing.

Social bonding is also encouraged within TTP. This can be in the form of providing support and peer reviews to other project leaders, or by honestly sharing stories of project successes and failures. The purpose is to create the identity of a project manager who is both professional and committed. For TTP, a professional manager is one who possesses a wide range of knowledge and has gained extensive experience. They have the skills to manage a project successfully. However, these skills need to be channelled towards a purpose and to forming a 'bridge' – a bond – with other people in the organisation. This includes a strong understanding of what the organisation and project stand for. The value of a sense of belonging should not be underestimated.

Reflection

How well do the following statements characterise your project? For each item, select one box only that best reflects your conclusion.

	Fully disagree		Neither agree nor disagree		Fully agree
We are reluctant to use single-point estimates.	I	2	3	4	5
We are reluctant to be overly optimistic.	I	2	3	4	5
We analyse interdependencies between risks and uncertainties.	I	2	3	4	5
	Fully disagree		Neither agree nor disagree		Fully agree
We appreciate risk and uncertainty beyond our immediate responsibilities.	I	2	3	4	5
We are constantly challenged on our 'big picture'.	I	2	3	4	5
We appreciate that traditional planning tools may amplify oversimplification.	I	2	3	4	5
	Fully disagree		Neither agree nor disagree		Fully agree
We challenge each other in our predictions.	I	2	3	4	5
We have plenty of time and space to challenge our estimates.	I	2	3	4	5
We convey to our stakeholders that our project is neither certain nor simple. It is complex.	I	2	3	4	5

Scoring: Add the numbers. If you score higher than 27, your capability to interpret risk and uncertainty is well developed. If you score 27 or lower, please think how you can address the issue of oversimplification.

References

1. Armour, P., Ten Unmyths of Project Estimation. *Communications of the ACM*, 2002. 45(11): p. 15–18.
2. Kahneman, D. and A. Tversky, Prospect Theory: An Analysis of Decision under Risk. *Econometrica*, 1979. 47(2): p. 263–92.
3. Hancock, D. and R. Holt, Tame, Messy and Wicked Problems in Risk Management, in *Working Paper Series*. 2003, Manchester Metropolitan University Business School Manchester.

4. Maylor, H.R., N.W. Turner, and R. Murray-Webster, How Hard Can It Be? *Research Technology Management*, 2013. 56(4): p. 45–51.

5. Meulbroek, L., A Better Way to Manage Risk. *Harvard Business Review*, 2001. 79(2): p. 22–4.

6. Klein, M., The Risk Premium for Evaluating Public Projects. *Oxford Review of Economic Policy*, 2000. 13(4): p. 29–42.

7. Hancock, D., *Tame, Messy and Wicked Risk Leadership*. 2010, Farnham: Gower.

8. Holt, R., Risk Management: The Talking Cure. *Organization*, 2004. 11(2): p. 251–70.

9. Walker, D., P. Steinfort, and T. Maqsood, Stakeholder Voices Through Rich Pictures. *International Journal of Managing Projects in Business*, 2014. 7(3): p. 342–61.

10. Checkland, P., *Systems Thinking, Systems Practice: A 30 Year Retrospective*. 1999, Chichester: John Wiley & Sons.

11. Bryson, J.M., F. Ackermann, C. Eden and C.B. Finn, *Visible Thinking: Unlocking Causal Mapping for Practical Business Results*, 2004: Chichester, John Wiley & Sons.

12. Lunenburg, F., Devil's Advocacy and Dialectical Inquiry: Antidotes to Groupthink. *International Journal of Scholarly Academic Intellectual Diversity*, 2012. 14(1): p. 1–9.

13. Conklin, J., *Wicked Problems and Social Complexity from Dialogue Mapping: Building Shared Understanding of Wicked Problems*. 2005, Hoboken, NJ: John Wiley & Sons.

14. Denning, S., Telling Tales. *Harvard Business Review*, 2004 (May): p. 1–8.

15. Kerzner, H. and F. Saladis, *Value-Driven Project Management*. 2009: Hoboken, NJ: John Wiley & Sons.

16. Flyvbjerg, B., M.K. Skamris Holm and S.r.L. Buhl, Inaccuracy in Traffic Forecasts. *Transport Reviews*, 2006. 26(1): p. 1–24.

17. Kemerer, C.F., Software Cost Estimation Models, in *Software Engineers Reference Handbook*, Anonymous, Editor. 1991, Surrey: Butterworth.

18. HM Treasury, *The Green Book: Appraisal and Evaluation in Central Government*. 2003, TSO: London.

19. MacDonald, M., *Review of Large Public Procurement in the UK*. 2002, HM Treasury: London.

20. Flyvbjerg, B., M.S. Holm and S. Buhl, Underestimating Costs in Public Works Projects: Error or Lie? *Journal of the American Planning Association*, 2002. 68(3): p. 279.

21. Schnaars, S.P., *Megamistakes: Forecasting and the Myth of Rapid Technological Change*. 1989: New York: Free Press.

22. Kutsch, E., H. Maylor, B. Weyer and J. Lupson, Performers, Trackers, Lemmings and the Lost: Sustained False Optimism in Forecasting Project Outcomes – Evidence From a Quasi-experiment. *International Journal of Project Management*, 2011. 29(8): p. 1070–81.

23. Abdel-Hamid, T.K., Impact of Schedule Estimation on Software Project Behaviour. *IEEE Software*, 1986. 3(4): p. 69–75.

24. Mumpower, L., Risk, Ambiguity, Insurance, and the Winner's Curse. *Risk Analysis*, 1991. 11: p. 519–22.

25. Thaler, R.H., Anomalies. *Journal of Economic Perspectives*, 1988. 2(1): p. 191–202.

26. Buehler, R. and D. Griffin, Planning, Personality, and Prediction: The Role of Future Focus in Optimistic Time Predictions. *Organizational Behavior and Human Decision Processes*, 2003. 92(1): p. 80.

27. Connolly, T. and D. Dean, Decomposed versus Holistic Estimates of Effort Required for Software Writing Tasks. *Management Science*, 1997. 43(7): p. 1029.

28. Morris, P.W.G. and G.H. Hough, *The Anatomy Of Major Projects*, 1987, Oxford: Major Projects Association.

29. De Meyer, A., C.H. Loch and M.T. Pich, Managing Project Uncertainty: From Variation to Chaos. *IEEE Engineering Management Review*, 2002. Third quarter: p. 91–8.

30. Flyvbjerg, B., From Nobel Prize to Project Management: Getting Risks Right. *Project Management Journal*, 2006. 37(3): p. 5–15.

31. Wachs, M., When Planners Lie With Numbers. *Journal of American Planning Association*, 1989. 55(4): p. 476–9.

32. Cliffe, L., M. Ramsay and D. Bartlett, *The Politics of Lying: Implications for Democracy*, 2000, London: Macmillan.

33. Flyvbjerg, B., N. Bruzelius and W. Rothengatter, *Megaprojects and Risk: An Anatomy of Ambition*, 2003, Cambridge: Cambridge University Press.

34. Yates, F.J., *Judgement and Decision Making*, 1990, New York: Prentice-Hall.

35. Flyvbjerg, B., Delusions of Success. *Harvard Business Review*, 2003. 81(12): p. 121–2.

36. Flyvbjerg, B., M. Garbuio and D. Lovallo, Delusion and Deception in Large Infrastructure Projects: Two Models for Explaining and Preventing Executive Disaster. *California Management Review*, 2009. 51(2): p. 170–93.

37. Lovallo, D. and D. Kahneman, Delusions of Success. *Harvard Business Review*, 2003. 81(7): p. 56–63.

38. Slovic, P., Perception of Risk. *Science*, 1987. 23: p. 280–5.

39. Slovic, P., B. Fischhoff, S. Lichtenstein, R.C. Schwing and W.A. Albers, Facts and Fears: Understanding Perceived Risk, in Anonymous (ed.) *Societal Risk Assessment*, 1980: New York, Plenum Press: p. 181–214.

40. Beierle, T.C., The Benefits and Costs of Disclosing Information About Risks: What Do We Know About Right-To-Know? *Risk Analysis,* 2004. 24(2): p. 335–46.

41. Sitkin, S.B. and L.R. Weingart, Determinants of Risky Decision-Making Behaviour: A Test of the Mediating Role of Risk Perceptions and Propensity. *Academy of Management Journal,* 1995. 38(6): p. 1573–92.

42. Royer, P.S., Risk Management: The Undiscovered Dimension of Project Management. *Project Management Journal,* 2000. 31(1): p. 6–13.

43. Weinstein, N.D., Unrealistic Optimism About Future Life Events. *Journal of Personality and Social Psychology,* 1980. 39: p. 806–20.

44. Pablo, A.L., Managerial Risk Interpretation: Does Industry Make a Difference? *Journal of Managerial Psychology,* 1999. 14(2): p. 92–108.

45. Jaafari, A., Management of Risks, Uncertainties and Opportunities on Projects: Time for a Fundamental Shift. *International Journal of Project Management,* 2001. 19: p. 89–101.

46. Jemison, D.B., Risk and the Relationship Among Strategy, Organizational Processes, and Performance. *Management Science,* 1987. 33(9): p. 1087–1101.

47. Krizan, Z. and P.D. Windschitl, The Influence of Outcome Desirability on Optimism. *Psychological Bulletin,* 2007. 133(1): p. 95–121.

Chapter 5
THE ART OF PREPARING

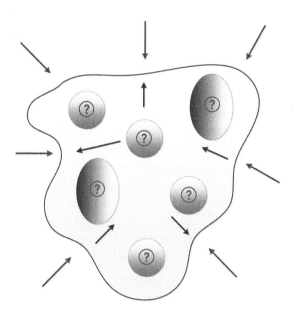

The environment of a project is not an empty shell but consists of the organisation, people, and ways of working. A structure needs to be set up for people to fit in, for ways of working to be established, all aligned to the goals of the project. The purpose is to notice more, interpret better and, ultimately, contain risk and uncertainty more appropriately.

The Lure of the Fail-safe

The main focus of preparing is often in the planning phase. Planning is, of course, a vital stage in any project. Careful planning allows the project team to establish an estimated cost and timescale for delivery of the project and, crucially, to think through the likely risks, uncertainties and complexities they will encounter as they undertake it. However, the temptation is to prepare ourselves only for what we know or suspect, and less for what we do not know or cannot yet imagine.

Preparing for the Expected

Planning for adversity often relies on traditional risk management. As outlined in Chapter 1, the risk management process involves identifying risks that might threaten the delivery of the project and finding ways to reduce or neutralise them. Typically, a process will be enacted whereby risks are identified and strategies put into place to tackle them. These strategies often include finding ways to eliminate the sources of risk, possibly transferring ownership of the problem to someone else (perhaps a supplier), reducing the possible impact of remaining risks to what might be regarded as acceptable (by putting in place contingency plans) and, finally, by accepting and seeking to manage the residual issues, should they emerge. In principle, this is fine; the project organisation can proceed, safe in the knowledge that risk is contained. The key problem with this is that the whole process of preparation is based on those risks that can be identified. How do project teams prepare for threats that have not even been considered (what we have called uncertainty)? The team engages with the project with confidence born of the knowledge that they have conducted a thorough risk management analysis – yet ignorant of the potentially ruinous areas of uncertainty that they may face. While they have prepared for what they know and understand, they are still vulnerable to the unexpected.

Erosion of Effectiveness

Many possible risks and uncertainties will, of course, never materialise. They may never have existed in the first place, or they were actually mitigated through management. The distinction between good management and good luck can sometimes be a fine line, though. This may lead to the temptation to 'cut corners' and reduce the extent of preparations. If the last few projects went well, this could be an opportunity to save time and money. The risks listed last time did not occur. Risk mitigation actions were undertaken; were they a waste of resources? The project team dutifully considers the list for a new project and some risks begin to be relegated. Perhaps these issues have never been experienced in the past, or have not occurred for a long time. Perhaps the project team members have been involved with a string of successful projects and begin to think that their projects are less risky than they first imagined. Clearly our team is particularly talented – those problems are more likely to affect others, not us. As a result, the risk analysis process slowly becomes a tick-box exercise – an activity that is followed because it is mandated or recommended. The nagging doubts fade, confidence grows. At the same time, pressure on resources encourages the project manager to seek opportunities for greater efficiency. Perhaps one way of freeing up resources, thereby taking the pressure off the budget, is to remove some of the activities directed at protecting the project from these risks that are thought never to have materialised.

Optimism Bias

Many managers, particularly project managers, are optimistic folk. Previously we argued that we tend to underestimate the extent of the adversity to which we are exposed. Making matters worse, we may also believe that our preparation covers more possible adversity than it actually does. As a result, we overestimate our preparatory state. In many respects, adopting a state of optimism is necessary for managers – they need to be confident that they are able to achieve their goals. However, without some reality check, there is a danger that managers become overly optimistic about their ability to reach their project's goals. There are a number of reasons for optimism bias. The first is the desired end-state and the tendency for managers to overestimate their control over events – the consequence of failing to take a systems view of the project. Next is thinking in terms of the particular (myself, my team, my project) rather than the general. Finally, a key reason for optimism bias is the amount of information available to project managers. In particular, project managers may feel they have taken all measures possible to plan for and handle risk in their projects but underestimate the ability of managers in other projects to do the same. As a result, they may feel that their project will avoid the risks and problems that beset other projects. This train of thought may not end well.

Abstracting Reality

The 'language' of project management consists to a great extent of written action plans, management guidance, instructions and procedures. Articulation is in the form of documents, booklets and manuals that can sit on a shelf unread and be forgotten about or, increasingly commonly, it resides in databases and on project management information systems. Risk becomes inchoate and opaque. Even if project workers can be persuaded to engage with the documentation and project management IT systems, they are often perceived as an abstraction from the day-to-day lived reality. Learning, and hence preparation, is arid and lacking in immediacy. There is no sense of getting 'close' to plans. Whereas the execution of plans – the act of containing adversity – stretches our senses and emotions, planning is 'dry', and can be mostly confined to documenting. This does not form a good platform for really understanding and perceiving adversity in the form of risk and uncertainty.

Rigidity over Flexibility

Organisational rigidity is very useful when it comes to imposing stability and discipline. This is often based on an analysis that considers past experiences and documents to be the mandated strategy (often from past successes, so this does have some justifiable rationale). The emphasis is on recognised structures, top-down governance and control systems, and prescribed processes and methods. This control is valuable as it ensures that people in the project know what they are doing and do not expose the project to unnecessary adversity through unexpected actions. In this way, the project can indeed be considered as prepared. However, rigidity itself has the potential to become a risk. Backward-looking procedures and processes stifle the flexibility needed to engage with the novelty and surprise that come with uncertainty. A pragmatic balance is hard to define and articulate within the project.

A Silo Mentality

In order to 'defend' a project from adversity, the tendency is often to increase the number of layers within it, both vertically and horizontally. Horizontally, we create silos of specialism and expertise; vertically, we add layers to a hierarchy in order to have dense, multi-layered defence mechanisms in place. What we tend to forget is that, by doing this, we can add complexity – and hence risk – to the project, and make the project more cumbersome. More silos imply more effort to overcome the inherent barriers, be they defined by specialism, ego, or status. Silos create barriers to communication, both in terms of how quickly information gets communicated and in its resultant interpretation by different specialisms. Similarly, specialist groups often form strong, cohesive bonds which encourage them to protect their own unit from risk and uncertainty, even if this is to the detriment of the overall project. It can create a dangerous 'us and them' attitude.

Anchoring

Projects are often planned in detail, in their entirety. The more we plan, the more we might get wedded to the plan. The purpose of planning is to try to transform uncertainty into certainty, and this is a good thing up until the point at which it turns into a self-fulfilling prophecy, whereby flexible solutions to emergent issues are rejected as they are not 'in the plan'. Planning to the edges of the risk horizon is fine. Going beyond can be dangerous.

Key Enablers to the Art of Preparing

Rigidity, inflexibility and complexity, built in through detailed planning, are situations we are frequently confronted with. This raises some difficult questions. For example, how much planning is actually 'enough'? When does (over)planning become a risk in itself? Although there are no clear answers to these questions, there are some enablers that can be considered in the planning stages in order to prepare a project for the adversity that comes with, in particular, uncertainty.

Faith

Preparing for adversity is a leap of faith. We must believe that our preparation has some positive effect on preventing adversity from destabilising our project. In advance of risk, uncertainty and complexity materialising, there will not be any proof of its effectiveness. Belief and confidence in the effectiveness of your preparation are therefore paramount.

A Wide Response Repository

One crucial aspect necessary in preparing for risk and uncertainty is a suitable set of skills across the project team that can be focused on any problem that might arise. This involves project staff and workers having not only the pertinent skills, but also ideally the ability to slot into each other's roles where necessary. This allows the team to develop a wide and effective response repository to deploy against any given situation. This is important as, to contain risks as they emerge, staff need to act quickly and with focus. Cross-training in a range of skills, beyond individuals' 'core' functions, helps create a built-in redundancy within projects. This excess of skills in the project team may not always be necessary or required (and indeed, it is likely to be a financial expense and possibly a drain on efficiency), until an unanticipated problem arises. It is at this time that the skills become crucial and the value of this investment becomes apparent.

As shown in Figure 5.1, the more 'traditional' approach to problem-solving is that decision power migrates to different sources of expertise – often defined by hierarchical position or status – until the particular problem is resolved. As a consequence, the nature of the difficulty may need to be conveyed and translated, often resulting in the loss of time and meaning on the way.

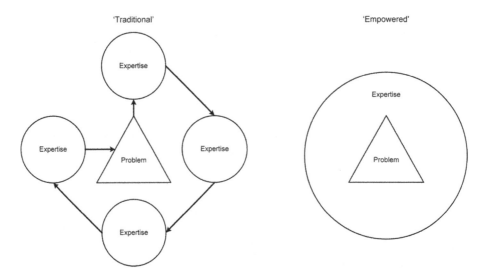

Figure 5.1   Empowerment beyond specialism

An alternative approach is to ensure that the people close to the problem are equipped to deal with it. To do this, they need a wide response repository to deal with any given problem, be it commercial, legal or technical. Escalations are only necessary when the boundaries of one's skill set are reached. However, in this respect, the number of escalations only shows how restricted one's response repository is. This, in itself, should be seen as a warning signal.

Of course, developing skill sets that span project teams is not easy. It requires the right people with a willingness to be empowered beyond their specialism, expertise and interest. It necessitates investment in training and support and a willingness to retain highly skilled individuals. Additionally, simulations, refresher-courses or job-sharing can be crucial in ensuring that skills do not ossify or become obsolete – which in itself leads to additional expenditure.

A by-product of this form of project organising is that project team members with different skills and specialisms can find that they overlap each other. This is the antithesis of the silo mentality – specialisms, status and egos are less likely to get in the way of tackling the problem at hand and this should benefit the project. This may require us to reconsider the nature of project efficiency. 'Local' efficiency – silos, expertise, tightly-controlled work packages – may indeed work well and appear financially prudent, on paper at least. However, 'broader' efficiency in terms of an effective response capability may prove superior when difficulties arise and can be resolved more swiftly.

BEST PRACTICE

The Power of Empowerment

It is not unusual at the beginning of a project to find that the client does not know exactly what they need. So project leaders must to be able to adapt:

> ... *half the job of the project leader is to find out what it is the client needs, not what he [or she] asks for.*

Project leaders need to be very flexible and, to this end, TTP has less focus on formal project management methods than might be expected. Instead the aim is to:

> ... *manage the people rather than the process.*

The requirement to adapt continually as projects progress means that the individual scientists and engineers are given the 'space' they require:

> *You are given a lot of responsibility but you are also given a lot of freedom ... you don't have managers telling you on a daily basis what to do, each person decides themselves what needs to be done.*

Project leaders at TTP are also given authority and a very high degree of autonomy:

> *We give a lot of responsibility to project leaders, not just for the technical leadership of the project. Ideally they have been involved in drawing up the proposal and developing a relationship before it evens starts. [Chairman]*

Project managers at TTP are empowered to make decisions regarding product development and customer service, and the extent of responsibility and authority given to them can be breath-taking:

> *We are all expected to do everything.*

From the cradle to grave of a project, managers are not simple executors of project management activities but take on a whole variety of roles, such as commercial, legal and project 'ownership', regardless of their original specialism. Such empowerment is by no means a comfortable proposition:

> *Oh, it is very scary, even now, even today.*

The benefits of empowerment are manifold, though. Project managers have a greater sense of purpose due to their extensive responsibility to look at a project from new and unfamiliar perspectives. This unfamiliarity, despite being uncomfortable, has the benefit of increasing their alertness and attention to problems that otherwise might remain hidden. Managers who extend their repertoire instead of delegating it to 'experts' see a situation with fresh eyes. They perceive more and are thus better positioned to notice and contain issues before they cascade into a crisis.

Seeing more and being able to put it together as a big picture helps to maintain oversight of project performance. It helps to address the issue of risk blindness that is so often a problem of centralised and 'specialist' project organisations. Going hand-in-hand with greater alertness and vigilance concerning the unexpected, project managers at TTP feel strongly attached to their projects and their organisation. Not only is their expertise valued but their skills in going beyond their expertise and initiative to push the envelope beyond what they are comfortable with are also highly valued.

It is acknowledged at TTP that there needs to be a balance between empowerment and traditional management. Empowerment, as valuable as it might be, comes with potential challenges. A few find the responsibility overwhelming (and may leave). All employees have to buy in to the system, which some may find uncomfortable. Devolving decision-making to someone who may not have the right information to make a good decision can be risky and the extra training required is another financial cost to be borne.

Senior management at TTP has to be sensitive to the needs of project managers as well as to the needs of the company and to know how to use a management style that will work best to achieve the desired outcomes. The principle of 'letting go' does not occur in a vacuum. A supportive culture (not to be confused with the traditional 'command and control' style) at TTP provides a 'safe' environment in which the responsibility of empowerment resting on a project manager's shoulders should not become a burden and a constraint.

Simulations, Games, Rehearsals

Just as airline pilots simulate many possibilities before getting into a real cockpit for the first time (and then regularly train on these and on new scenarios throughout their careers), so too can project workers prepare themselves for adversity in their projects. Naturally, the nature of the simulation will vary from context to context and project to project but simulations, focused on the unexpected and on hitherto unexperienced possibilities, are perfectly feasible in almost all project settings.

The purpose of simulations, games or rehearsals is to get people close to adversity with the intention of encouraging understanding of the varied nature of risk and uncertainty, but in a safe environment. Understanding adversity that has not yet materialised through reading some form of documentation is limited in its effectiveness. Words are not enough. If we want to understand and prepare ourselves better for what lies in wait we need to practice it, and receive immediate feedback on our performance.

Getting 'close' to adversity can be achieved through various means, such as role-plays, or entirely new scenarios can be devised with project staff being given different roles to take on – this is an excellent way to help project team members begin to understand the perspective of different stakeholders. For example, how and why might staff resist a major organisational change? Why do protestors resist major infrastructure projects? How did the Challenger project team begin to normalise risk so that NASA's culture of safety was allowed to become degraded? Many organisations also train their staff on computer-based simulations where poor choices have no negative consequences in the real world but provide powerful experiences that can be drawn upon in future projects.

Routine-flexibility

Routines are valuable in stable, secure and repeatable environments in that they ensure consistency of output. However, projects are often anything but stable. The idea of imposing rules and procedures on an environment in flux may be counterproductive. A way of limiting flux and creating the conditions for stability is to try to close the project off from outside influences. However, protecting it from changes by stakeholders and keeping risk out may also mean inhibiting the possibility of enhancing value. For example, 'protecting' the project might mean preventing stakeholders, such as end-users, from getting involved in explaining what they really want, especially when the project is underway. So, although boundaries (see Figure 5.2) around the project might protect the key deliverables by limiting opportunities for change, they also mean that the project is less likely to deliver exactly what the end-users actually need. If sponsors and funders are to draw maximum value from the project, then they will have to require project teams to allow them to get involved. This, in turn, exposes the project to the possibility of ongoing change and with that comes additional risk and uncertainty. Rigid routines may collapse in this kind of environment, so what is really required in projects is a degree of flexibility to adjust to the possibility of an ever-changing environment.

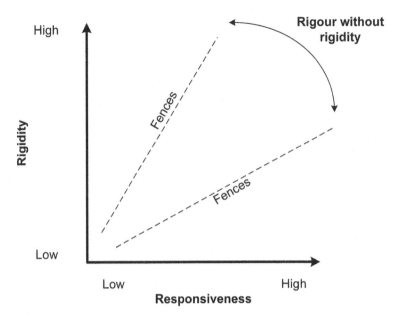

Figure 5.2   Freedom with fences

Flexibility, though, can be dangerous. Too much can become counterproductive, so project teams require latitude to be flexible yet must not lose sight of the rules and procedures that allow the project to keep on track. This concept was articulated at Harley Davidson and is sometimes known as 'freedom with fences' [1]. By adopting this approach, project members not only have the freedom to 'push back' where this might be required, but this very flexibility itself should become a routine, a kind of (dynamic) capability. Flexibility itself becomes the routine mindset. This approach needs to be understood and embedded in the organisational culture of the project team from the start, meaning that whenever risk and uncertainty emerge, the project workers are immediately able to loosen their 'normal' operating practices and respond with innovative and imaginative solutions.

In this way, routine-flexibility is not the contradiction in terms that it may at first seem to be. It can be argued [2] that organisational routines require agency on the part of people working in the organisation and that, with this, comes subjectivity and power. Routines are produced by many people with different preferences, amounts of information, and interpretations. This situation provides scope not only for stability, but also for flexibility and change within organisations. Routines are the default position and provide boundaries within which flexibility can be exercised. Essentially, it is a matter of releasing the flexibility aspect and allowing it free rein, but within defined constraints –

'fences'. Patrolling the fences (the limits of freedom) is the job of the project leader, who takes a strategic perspective on the project goals and ensures that changes enacted within the project in the face of risk and uncertainty do not unduly threaten the project outcomes.

WHAT THE LITERATURE SAYS ABOUT …

Routines

Routines are a central feature of all human organisations. They are the means by which organisations achieve most of what they do. They can been defined as *'repetitive, recognizable patterns of interdependent actions, carried out by multiple actors'* [2, p. 95] and take the form of repeated habits and behaviours that characterise much of what people undertake in the workplace. They provide stability and continuity, set out the basis for accountability and enable organisations to arrange expertise and power relationships efficiently.

However, Feldman and Pentland [2], drawing on Latour's [3] work of performance in everyday life in organisations, highlight the distinction between the 'ostensive' (the abstract pattern that guides action) and 'performative' aspects, which might vary every time a routine is enacted. They argue that although the concept of routines suggests the notion of a stable, conforming and compliant system, routines are actually continuously changing [4, 5] and are generative [6]. What this means is that, over time, some patterns of action (routines) are retained and preserved while others fall away, either through changes in policy or simply from lack of use, with no consequences. Routines become generative where they enable the organisation to achieve its critical tasks. However, where routines become embedded due to inertia and habit rather than their ability to help achieve the goals of the organisation, they can be seen as sclerotic and a barrier to improvement.

An interesting aspect of routines in organisations is that their enactment will frequently come with secondary, often unexpected outcomes. These outcomes may well be suboptimal, leading to inefficiency for the organisation. Vaughan [7, p.274] argues that adverse outcomes are often *'a routine by-product of the characteristics of the system itself'*, caused by factors she and others have suggested can include mistakes and misconduct [7], the non-adoption of practices that have been shown to be effective elsewhere [8], the adoption of practices that work effectively in one context but do not fit local conditions and the blind adherence to habitual practice [9], practices that are enacted mindlessly [10], practices that become decoupled and 'drift' from written procedure [11], and rule violations and discrepant practices that accumulate unnoticed [12].

While individual failures are unlikely to derail a project or programme, their accumulation can, over time, erode the system [13]. Because routines are part of human experience, enacted by human beings who will frequently behave in unexpected, sometimes seemingly irrational and inefficient ways, perhaps for their own agendas or even on a whim, ever tighter controls through activities like risk management and compliance are not a fully adequate solution. They will not preclude failure (at least in the long term) but could have the effect of stifling and expunging innovation and freedom to act. This is especially true in complex project work [14], where there is no single 'process' solution.

What this means is that routines are not static, but influenced by changes in the organisational environment. It also means that the controls and demands for compliance cannot be relied upon to eliminate failure. Routines are performed and this performance will frequently deviate from the ostensive routine, perhaps with detrimental effects.

A Sensible Planning Horizon

Given that a planning process will be undertaken in almost all projects, a key issue will be the length of the planning horizon. The project planning horizon is the period of time covered by detailed, articulated and actionable plans. Clearly, some aspects of project planning will cover the entire project period but, with regard to risk planning, preparation should be confined to what one can confidently predict, as anything beyond the 'risk horizon' is largely uncertain. The problem with longer-term risk plans is that they can become self-fulfilling prophesies, with contingencies and estimates allocated for events that are expected to happen. The question then becomes 'what is a good planning horizon'? The answer is that this is entirely contingent on the nature of the project and, crucially, on the degree of uncertainty in the external and internal project environment. This is, to a certain extent, a matter of judgement. The risk horizon can be extended if it is deemed prudent to do so. However, although this might be desirable, it carries the risk of complacency, with project staff assuming that future risks have been accounted for and need not require attention and vigilance on their part. Estimates may go unchallenged and reduced vigilance invites residual uncertainty.

Goal Flexibility

One aspect of risk that sometimes gets forgotten is the alternative view of risk and uncertainty as opportunities actually to add value to the project. Instead of just considering the negative implications, it can make sense to seek flexibility in the project goals and try to turn threats into opportunities. For example, regular planning iterations (a concept associated with Agile project management) allow goals to be reassessed repeatedly, expectations to be managed and learning from previous iterations to be incorporated. Each iteration is allowed to influence the next, and this process is quite transparent. This ability to be flexible with targets allows both for risks to be addressed and for opportunities to be incorporated. This is not suitable for every project but, even where stakeholders are quite clear on the outcomes and benefits they want from the work, a door remains open to amend those goals in light of new knowledge.

WHAT THE LITERATURE SAYS ABOUT ...

Flexibility

Often seen as the obverse of organisational routines, organisational flexibility is not a straightforward concept and frequently runs into issues around definition. In its broadest sense, flexibility can be seen as the capacity to adapt to change in the environment [15] but even within a single organisation, different types of flexibility and inflexibility may exist simultaneously. Specifically, Evans [16] identifies four areas or dimensions of organisational flexibility:

1. **Temporal dimension**
   - The length of time it takes for an organisation to respond to changes in the environment.
2. **Range dimension**
   - A flexible firm has the ability to adapt to ensure its continued viability. This can be done both by planning for events that are likely to occur (foreseeable) and by adapting to circumstances in the face of the unpredictable (unforeseeable).
3. **Intention dimension**
   - This dimension of flexibility concerns the degree to which organisations take an offensive (proactive) or defensive (reactive) approach to flexibility. In the former, organisations seek to control change, whereas in the latter they are simply responding to change.
4. **Focus dimension**
   - There are two types of flexibility: internal and external. Internal flexibility focuses on those aspects of an organisation within its immediate domain (e.g. production processes, employees, organisational structures) while external flexibility is concerned with aspects beyond an organisation's immediate control (e.g. suppliers, alliances, multinational operations).

Clearly, an organisation can avail itself of many sorts of flexibility and having flexibility of all types is generally desirable.

Flexibility is a well-known concept in the literature [17]. Sayer [18] argues that organisations have always combined flexibility and inflexibility and that recent observations are merely new versions of previous ideas, rather than a clear trend towards necessarily greater flexibility. Something else that should be considered is that, while flexibility is often regarded as a 'good thing', it is not cost-free. Flexibility has costs in terms of resources and reduced efficiency as well as possible hidden costs of increased employee stress and a reduction in organisational focus [19]. Nevertheless, it is increasingly seen as crucial to organisations, generally in terms of maintaining their competitiveness. From the perspective of projects and their inherent uncertainty, some degree of flexibility can be considered essential.

Ironically, Lenfle and Loch [20] have observed that as organisations around the world and in industries of all types have sought to capture the innovation and creativity that flexibility can bring them in order to maintain their competitive edge, by contrast project directors and managers have sought to impose ever tighter control on projects, relegating the project discipline to an 'order taker niche' rather than positioning it centre-stage as a creator of strategic value for organisations.

Again, given the uncertainty, complexity and risk inherent in projects, although project leaders frequently seek to impose the control Lenfle and Loch described on projects, in reality flexibility must be accommodated. Lenfle and Loch [20] argued that because flexibility was always going to be required, project leaders may as well plan for it rather than allowing a tension between control and flexibility to emerge, with flexibility being accommodated in an inefficient and less effective manner *post hoc*.

Leading the Art of Preparing

Risk and uncertainty can emerge at any time, in any form, from any source. The project team needs to be prepared to deal with whatever might happen. It needs to be vigilant in looking for the weak signals as they begin to emerge, alert to threats, and alive to opportunities. It is both difficult and counterproductive to seal the project off from its environment in the hope of 'keeping risk out', and equally problematic (and more than likely, ineffective) to tighten rules and procedures in the hope of eliminating project failure.

Preparation begins with standard risk procedures (routines) being put in place but it is dangerous to leave things there in the hope that this covers all eventualities. The risk register should be just a starting point – there are a number of risks which will have been missed or downgraded, together with a host of uncertainties. It is incumbent on the project leader to create a sense of readiness among the project team, so that they are not just ready for the expected but appreciate the threat of the unexpected. This means empowering the project team, providing the freedom and latitude to act, and creating a culture of communication by removing the barriers that might prevent this, thereby enhancing flexibility.

Maintaining Goal Flexibility

If project iterations are implemented, a key aspect is not simply to progress to the next iteration but to ensure that a short phase of reflection occurs. Seeking to learn from the previous output and considering how this may influence the overall goal is valuable. These short but intense reflection periods may include questioning how the experience of the completed iteration influences the project delivery process and what that means for the overarching project goal. It is a reflection of how value (see Chapter 4) evolves. As a result, it is important to communicate and sensitise people to the idea that nothing is necessarily set in stone and that the learning from an iteration informs subsequent iterations.

Empowering Project Members

Exhorting project managers/leaders to empower workers and staff to act on their own initiative can be difficult. There are two general problems: that the leader is reluctant to lose what they perceive as control; and that workers are reluctant to take responsibility. From the leader's point of view, a transformational model can be far more effective than a transactional model (see What the Literature says about Leadership). Transactional leaders focus primarily on role supervision, organisation and compliance, paying attention to work performed in order to spot faults and deviations. Transformational leaders focus more on being a role model, inspiring and keeping workers interested, challenging project workers to take greater ownership for their work, and understanding their strengths and weaknesses.

For transformational project leaders, empowerment can be prompted in a number of ways:

- To encourage on-the-spot feedback so that issues are communicated quickly and action can be taken immediately. The ground rules for such feedback need to be clearly set – it must be both constructive and respectful. Essentially, the project team must trust its leader and each other to deliver honest and helpful praise and criticism.

- Project leaders can adopt an 'executive mentality' and approach. Hosting regular meetings with their teams and sharing with them the happenings within the organisation help the teams understand the main goals they are driving towards. Giving them a rundown on how other projects or parts of the organisation are performing makes it easier for them to adopt this mindset.
- It is important to present project workers with new challenges and opportunities so they can demonstrate and achieve their full potential.
- Although project workers should be encouraged to embrace new experiences, they cannot be pushed too far out of their comfort zones or the experience will become a negative one. Their boundaries must be respected. It is the job of the project leader to recognise and understand this.
- Empowered project workers need to have some control over how they direct their work. This means having the freedom to express flexibility and creativity. It also means that project workers will act on their own initiative, but this flexibility needs to be within limits (freedom with fences), which must be explained to project staff.
- Giving up control and empowering a project team might feel like a very uncomfortable experience for many project leaders who are used to a more transactional model of control and compliance. The temptation is to watch the workers' every move but, in monitoring someone closely, their ability to grow, learn and build confidence to take action is impeded. The project workers need to be given space and need to be trusted.

Breaking Down Barriers

The way to break down barriers between silos is twofold. First, try and reduce the number of hierarchical levels, so that communication can flow more rapidly. Think of the flattest hierarchy possible. Second, empowerment in itself reduces the need for in-depth silos of expertise. Instead, 'wider' silos with extended insight and responsibility can be created. 'Generalists' can work as effective conduits of expertise between specialists, since they have broader (but shallower) domain knowledge and can be effective 'boundary-spanners'.

This, though, is a rather structural option to breaking down barriers, which may take more subtle, behavioural forms. Culturally, egos and status may prevent the rapid flow of information. One way to overcome this is to work so that decision-making is driven by those who are the closest to the problem and have the greatest expertise to deal with it (see Chapter 6, Deferring to Expertise).

In terms of geographically distributed (or virtual) teams, it is important to promote some social interaction. Encourage people to meet or, if that is not possible, at least try to make sure they can see each other. Personal, real-time communication helps build trust and effective working relationships between non-co-located staff.

Helping People to get 'Close' to Risk

Organisations are comfortable investing significant resources in ensuring that computer simulations are carried out on the technical aspects of engineering projects, especially where there is a risk of catastrophic failure that could lead to loss of life or significant cost. As a result, engineering elements are carefully designed and rarely fail. However, the kind of simulations, role-playing and games which would be useful to prepare project workers for the 'soft' risks of stakeholder interaction and behaviour are rarely undertaken outside a business school environment. Even where training like this does occur, it is normally in a sterile classroom setting.

The project leader is responsible for ensuring that the project team is prepared to tackle risk and one way of preparing them is to undertake case studies and role-plays. Although it is often difficult, the project leader should try to find the time and resources to ensure that the project team has the opportunity to participate in these kinds of simulations and, in so doing, gets 'close' to risk in a tangible and memorable way.

Role-plays, in particular, can fill participants with dread but some simple procedures can help ensure that the whole process goes smoothly and that the participants feel they are learning and getting close to risk and uncertainty. These are:

- *Objectives*. The leader needs to be clear about why the role-play is being undertaken, whether it is being assessed in some way and whether the activity is being tailored for different skills and experience.
- *Timing*. Is the role-play to be a one-off experience or is it part of a broader risk analysis/management activity? Frequently, it is held at the end of a training session or management activity with the idea that participants are then able to apply lessons learnt.
- *Briefing*. People need to be clear about what they are supposed to do. This should be supported by sufficient time to prepare, rather than just being rushed into a scenario.

- *Observation and feedback.* Observers can be hugely beneficial to participants' learning and observation should be encouraged.

In summary, role-play events should be focused and clear. The participants should be able to see the relevance to their project and take their learning back to the workplace.

BEST PRACTICE

Training

Project Management training is often related purely to conveying hard skills, such as how to apply processes and procedures. Although such training is beneficial and provides a project leader at TTP with a set of tools, TTP's 'Project Leadership Programme' also emphasises the soft side of leading a project:

> The project leadership course is opening people's eyes to the tools that are available to them to deal with things and actually also their freedom to use them, not to assume constraints but actually they can make a difference ...

The 'hard' focus of training involves familiarisation with traditional 'waterfall' planning approaches such as Gantt Charts and Risk Management. However, most of the time is spent on contextualising:

- leadership;
- conflict management;
- stakeholder/relationship management;
- time management;
- motivation.

Of great importance in this leadership programme is the manner in which it is conveyed, and a variety of methods are used to present learning material. These include TTP-specific case studies, role-playing, exercises and in-class simulations. This maintains the attention of training participants. Feedback is provided on a regular basis and participants engage in the exchange of ideas with each other and the facilitators. The training programme is divided into small 'doses', so delegates do not become overwhelmed. Acquired knowledge is then immediately applied in the form of interactive applied sessions. Finally, a key factor is that the training programmes are designed to be interesting and entertaining.

Incentivising Beyond Compliance

The reward and incentive scheme has to reinforce the open flow of communication required of the project team as well as support an open and ongoing discussion of project purpose. There are a number of techniques the project leader can utilise to encourage the kind of focus required [21]:

- Use interviews and focus groups to ensure the real goals of the project are understood and shared.
- Review the reward and incentive procedures from the standpoint of balancing long-term project reliability with short-run delivery targets.
- Develop and reward risk and uncertainty identification activities and include these in staff evaluation.

The reward and incentive process needs to focus on both the intrinsic and extrinsic motivation of project workers. The former refers to motivation based on the work itself. Here, providing project members with greater autonomy and latitude to act, with fewer process and procedural constraints, is in itself a powerful motivator. The extrinsic rewards are in terms of financial and status outcomes. This reward system should be focused on communication and vigilance – supporting resilience – rather than just on speedy, efficient activity which may be too focused on the smaller, short-term picture.

The Impact of Preparing on Relationships

The preparations for delivering a resilient project system are not necessarily confined to the immediate project team. Any suppliers or contractors also need to be ready and to be brought into the preparation processes. Complacency because they 'think' they are prepared is as dangerous for these stakeholders as it is for central project team members. Equally, external suppliers need to have a sense of the 'big picture' and be incentivised to communicate and be vigilant.

One aspect of preparation is dealing with the issues of power and politics. For this, attention also needs to be turned to other stakeholders: funders; sponsors; possibly end-users – in short, those stakeholders who could be particularly influential. As much as the project delivery team needs to be prepared for uncertainty that may arise as the project progresses, so too stakeholders must be made aware that they themselves are a source of that uncertainty and that they also need to think through their involvement and activity in the project.

They should be encouraged to focus on the 'big picture' as much as the little details, and also be alert to the weak, early signs of emerging risk and uncertainty.

Integrating Stakeholders in Preparations

Just as the project team should be involved in preparations for resilience, so too should key stakeholders. In many ways, the same issues apply – they need to guard against complacency, be ready to be flexible and to let go of constraining procedures when uncertainty emerges. They should understand the big picture and be motivated to communicate and reflect frequently. Perhaps the key problem here is motivation. Suppliers and contractors are usually engaged, and their involvement specified, by contract. They are also likely to be experienced. They might legitimately ask why they need to worry about all these issues of preparation – for them, risk is normalised and confidence abounds. Perhaps the key way of encouraging involvement in the process is through appropriate incentives, but then the funders need to understand that suppliers must be properly paid (or otherwise rewarded, perhaps with repeat work) for engaging with a process of preparation for resilience.

BEST PRACTICE

AVIVA

Establishing Long-term Commitment

Projects are temporary endeavours and so too is the commitment to them. Engagement and dedication often do not extend beyond the duration of the work as people move on. Frequently, short-term and, in particular, long-term outcomes of a project become forgotten or are scrutinised by outsiders – external assessors (whose expertise the project participants may question) who were not involved in the delivery of the project.

Aviva has sought to overcome this. The typical detachment and lack of long-term commitment to a project that many organisations see is countered by committing key decision-makers to the long-term benefits beyond the duration of their project implementation. It all starts with the sponsor. A sponsor at Aviva is a functional manager – usually a Director – for whom the project is expected to have a positive effect. The sponsor will bid for a project by developing a business case, to be scrutinised by an independent panel:

> *The idea of the bank manager model is that if someone wants a project to happen, they need to be prepared to sponsor it but not just for the short term of getting that project up and running and implemented but also for at least two years after implementation so that the benefits are realised.*

Such a business case outlines the traditional short-term outputs of a project (i.e. time, budget, specification) but also asks the sponsor to define outcomes that should apply two years after the end of the project. Some examples of these outcomes might include:

- increased efficiency in operations;
- reduction of legal vulnerability;
- improved public image.

The sponsor and the project manager share a collective responsibility to deliver both project outputs and outcomes, as they are intrinsically built on each other. Challenges are jointly addressed by the project manager and sponsor:

> *So, for example, if I [as the project manager] suddenly hit a brick wall on my project and I need extra resources and all the IT teams are saying to me we don't have any extra resources, then I'll go to my sponsor and explain that if the delivery is to continue, they will need to intervene to sort the issue out.*

A key challenge is that these long-term outcomes are often difficult to measure and predict precisely so far ahead of their implementation:

> *They are defined by the sponsor for that specific piece of work, so the sponsor could say 'I want to bring in this piece of work and this is the benefit it's going to give,' so it could be if we do this then we will increase our sales by X amount over a two year period or we will cut our costs by X amount over the two year period.*

They tend to be measured subjectively by approximation. To address uncertainty in estimating these outcomes, some are defined with the help of ranges – from-to approximations.

At Aviva, the sponsor is committed to the longer-term, often difficult to measure, outcomes while the project manager concentrates on delivering the more specific short-term outputs. In particular, this arrangement drives the engagement of the sponsor in the project as well as in transferring short-term outputs into long-term outcomes. This form of engagement is further underlined by the impact of not achieving (or exceeding) initially-defined outputs and outcomes. Both the sponsor's and the project manager's future prospects, including the type of projects they can sponsor or manage, are in play and there is an emphasis on incentivising the exploitation of opportunities to deliver something better, faster and at less cost next time:

> *There will be an impact on what sorts of things they're allowed to sponsor or manage in the future, there's the credibility …*

Addressing Discomfort

Goal flexibility, and the commensurate implications for the planning process, may well be uncomfortable for stakeholders, despite the positive implications for responding to risk and uncertainty. The idea of ever-shifting goalposts and using diverse ways to accomplish the project is difficult to justify. If not addressed, there is a possibility that the project manager will simply be labelled a 'bad planner'. Stakeholders need to understand why the planning horizon is shortened and need to be guided through the logic. The project leader should offer advice, transparency and clarity about the planned state of a project, as well as about its actual progress. It is the client, though, who should provide frequent feedback on which the project leader's decisions are ultimately based.

BEST PRACTICE

AVIVA

Winning Hearts and Minds

The commitment of stakeholders to buy in to a project is not solely driven by the project brief or by a contract that has been signed off. Central to committing people to a project is trust and respect:

> 'Usually [we listen to] their questions, their concerns, their objections and often it boils down to the fact that they didn't really understand why they were being asked to do it and they didn't have time. So you find them some resource, you help them have the time, you talk to the manager if necessary and get them the time but more importantly you make sure they understand why they're doing this because if they understand it, even if they do not totally agree with it, they're more likely to do it.'

Listening to, and understanding, stakeholders' objectives and concerns and managing their need to have a greater understanding of what the project is all about helps to ensure that everyone is on the same page. At Aviva, project leaders do not listen solely in order to understand but do so to help develop trust with the stakeholder, not just to convey the message but also to turn that stakeholder into a messenger. The project leader delivering that message must:

- allow time to listen to stakeholders, being careful not cut off a discussion because of other obligations;
- allow face-to-face discussion and personal interaction to allow social bonding;

- minimise external distractions by focusing attention on what is being said;
- keep an open mind;
- ask questions to clarify and to show enthusiasm about the message and the messenger.

Listening, *per se*, makes Aviva stakeholders 'worthy' – appreciated, of interest and valued. This is paid back as openness towards what the project stands for and how it affects them. However, listening needs to be followed by converting this openness into trust, a belief that the message – the project – is for the good of oneself *and* other beneficiaries. This depends upon credibility being established by providing honest feedback on the discussions. 'How are concerns addressed?', 'How can objectives be aligned?', 'What questions help build up credibility?' At Aviva, the action of establishing credibility is supported by 'evidence', be it benchmarks, case studies, or comparable projects where something similar has worked. Working together and finding compromises helps build credibility and allows trust to blossom.

Towards an Art of Preparing

This chapter has been about resisting the temptation to prepare a project for a single, most likely future. Risk and uncertainty mean that this is unwise. Rather, a project needs to be prepared for multiple futures, accepting the uncertainty that lies beyond the risk horizon. Providing an extensive repository of options, empowering people beyond their specialisms, breaking down barriers and silos between people, and the integrative role of stakeholders in exploiting this flexibility is paramount. Hence, resilience is not just an outcome of accurate and precise planning for the expected; it is an outcome of preparing a project for the unexpected.

Reflection

How well do the following statements characterise your project? For each item, select one box only that best reflects your conclusion.

	Fully disagree		Neither agree nor disagree		Fully agree
We believe in the effectiveness of our management of risk and uncertainty, although we have no proof.	1	2	3	4	5
The goal of the project is not set in stone but can be influenced by what we learn throughout the project.	1	2	3	4	5
We experience risk and uncertainty before it happens, and don't just plan for it.	1	2	3	4	5
	Fully disagree		**Neither agree nor disagree**		**Fully agree**
Project members have an extensive skill set that enables them to act on uncertainty.	1	2	3	4	5
We are equipped with a wide ranging freedom to act, beyond process.	1	2	3	4	5
We are trained beyond our specialism.	1	2	3	4	5
	Fully disagree		**Neither agree nor disagree**		**Fully agree**
People can rely on each other without many barriers to overcome.	1	2	3	4	5
We share the discomfort of risk and uncertainty with our stakeholders.	1	2	3	4	5
Our stakeholders are part of the preparation.	1	2	3	4	5

Scoring: Add the numbers. If you score higher than 27, your capability to prepare for uncertainty and complexity is good. If you score 27 or lower, please think of how you can enhance your state of preparedness.

References

1.   Stenzel, J., Freedom with Fences: Robert Stephens Discusses CIO Leadership and IT Innovation, in *CIO Best Practices: Enabling Strategic Value with Information Technology*, J. Stenzel (ed.), 2010, SAS Institute Inc.: Cary, NC.

2. Feldman, M.S. and B.T. Pentland, Reconceptualizing Organizational Routines as a Source of Flexibility and Change. *Administrative Science Quarterly*, 2003. 48(1): p. 94–118.

3. Latour, B., Visualization and Cognition: Thinking with Eyes and Hands, in *Knowledge and Society Studies in the Sociology of Culture Past and Present* H. Kuklick (ed.) 1986, Jai Press London. p. 1–40.

4. Weick, K.E. and R.E. Quinn, Organizational Change and Development. *Annual Review of Pyschology*, 1999. 50(1): p. 361–88.

5. Tsoukas, H. and R. Chia, On Organizational Becoming: Rethinking Organizational Change. *Organization Science*, 2002. 13(5): p. 567–82.

6. Pentland, B.T. and H.H. Reuter, Organizational Routines as Grammars of Action. *Administrative Science Quarterly*, 1994. 39(3): p. 484–510.

7. Vaughan, D., The Dark Side of Organizations: Mistake, Misconduct, and Disaster. *Annual Review of Sociology*, 1999. 25: p. 271–305.

8. Pascale, R., *Managing on the Edge*. 1990, New York: Simon and Schuster.

9. Weick, K.E., The Collapse of Sensemaking in Organizations: The Mann Gulch Disaster. *Administrative Science Quarterly*, 1993. 38(4): p. 628–52.

10. Langer, E.J., *The Power of Mindful Learning*. 1997, Reading, MA: Addison-Wesley.

11. Snook, S.A., *Friendly Fire: The Accidental Shootdown of US Black Hawks over Northern Iraq*. 2000, Oxford: Princeton University Press.

12. Turner, B.A., The Organizational and Interorganizational Development of Disasters. *Administrative Science Quarterly*, 1976. 21(3): p. 318–97.

13. Reason, J., *Human Error*. 1990, Cambridge: Cambridge University Press.

14. Maylor, H.R., N.W. Turner and R. Murray-Webster, How Hard Can It Be? *Research Technology Management*, 2013. 56(4): p. 45–51.

15. Golden, W. and P. Powell, Towards a Definition of Flexibility: In Search of the Holy Grail? *Omega*, 2000. 28: p. 373–84.

16. Evans, J.S., Strategic Flexibility for High Technology Manoeuvres: A Conceptual Framework. *Journal of Management Studies*, 1991. 28(1): p. 69–89.

17. Kotha, S., Mass Customization: Implementing the Emerging Paradigm for Competitive Advantage. *Strategic Management Journal*, 1995. 16(S1): p. 21–42.

18. Sayer, A., Postfordism in Question. *International Journal of Urban and Regional Research*, 1989. 13(4): p. 666–95.

19. Das, T.K. and B. Elango, Managing Strategic Flexibility: Key to Effective Performance. *Journal of General Management*, 1995. 20(3): p. 60–75.

20. Lenfle, S. and C. Loch, Lost Roots: How Project Management Came to Emphasize Control Over Flexibility and Novelty. *California Management Review*, 2010. 53(1): p. 32–55.

21. Roberts, K.H., R. Bea and D.L. Bartles, Must Accidents Happen? Lessons from High Reliability Organizations. *The Academy of Management Executive,* 2001. 15(3): p. 70–79.

Chapter 6
THE ART OF CONTAINING

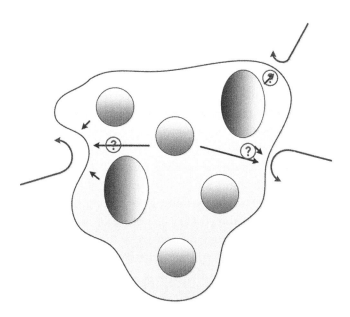

Your project is prepared and is equipped with the necessary flexibility to engage with adversity. The next step is to develop a commitment to contain risk and uncertainty appropriately, and to prevent complexity from cascading into a full-blown crisis. Each part of the project must be ready to work together coherently to align the execution of responses with the problems at hand as and when they arise. Nevertheless, some sub-units in your project will need support to counter each problem. They cannot always just act on their own. Collective ownership goes hand-in-hand with collective accountability, yet this also needs to work in tandem with individual responsibility to act on risks and uncertainties. It is a delicate balance.

The Lure of Control

The preparation for your project is done. Not only is the project prepared for the expected – risk – but also for the unexpected – uncertainty. The project is in a state of alertness, with participants constantly on the lookout for what might go wrong. Their preparedness goes beyond what one normally expects; their readiness to act quickly offers a timely resolution, before issues can cascade into a crisis. Yet, as with all actions, there are behavioural obstacles that may make this state of readiness less effective.

Habitual Responses

All projects involve some kind of journey into the unknown. Even fairly routine projects incorporate uncertainty to some degree, since all projects necessarily involve some element of novelty. Projects that are technologically and socially complex involve a host of uncertainties. Faced with these challenges, the temptation for many managers is to fall back on 'tried and tested' routines and rely on these until it is, perhaps, too late. Where no problems emerge, this behaviour is fine. It is when things start to go awry that reflexively following procedures or routines that have been used successfully before can become a problem. Indeed, it may be that responses to problems are habitual – if something goes wrong, then certain routines are followed, regardless of the context or nature of the problem. Of course, the main problem with habitual responses is that they are the antithesis of effective learning. They are an attempt to find a ready-made answer to any problem, when in practice these new difficulties often require more innovative and imaginative solutions.

Hierarchical Escalation

Where managers encounter problems, there is often a tendency to ask someone more senior to take the crucial decision on how to respond. Frequently, this is not about what action should be taken, but more about passing accountability for decision-making up the hierarchy. This is not always a problem and it is frequently necessary where there are crucial decisions to be made which may lie outside the control or scope of the project manager (for example, resource allocation across a portfolio of projects). However, where it is related to tackling risks, escalation can present major problems. This is because escalation of decision-making is slow – it requires the project manager to articulate and communicate the problem clearly to senior management, for people at a more senior level to understand the nature and implications of the problem and then for a decision to be made and communicated. Managers at a more senior level are generally more remote and removed from the project situation and may often, therefore, not be best placed to make decisions in any case. In the time it takes to make a decision, the risky circumstances may well have escalated into something far more problematic for the project and this could have been avoided if the people closest to the problem had dealt with it straightaway. Other, slightly subtler issues arise, too. If a reporting and escalation culture takes root, then any problems or deviations from plan can result in excessive reporting (for example, daily conference calls being set up), resulting in extensive effort to measure and report rather than actually to fix the problem. This can be painful, and may well cause managers to 'hide' small problems until they can resolve them themselves in order to avoid extra scrutiny. The upshot of this, of course, is that the first senior management hear of these problems is when they have become full-blown crises that can no longer be concealed.

The problem of inappropriate escalation generally lies in a lack of empowerment on the part of those working where problems are occurring. If they feel unable or unwilling to be accountable for their actions, they will defer decisions rather than take action when it is needed.

Problem of Accountability

The tendency to escalate problems through the organisational hierarchy is closely related to the issue of accountability. Who is accountable for decision-making and what are the consequences of making a mistake? Where there is a lack of empowerment in the project team, decisions will always be deferred or escalated. This results in a delay in decision-making and, in turn, allows risks to escalate. The problem lies with people retreating to compliance. If they have 'ticked the box', their job is secure. Compliance becomes a tool for protecting individuals rather than serving the best interests of the project. This goes to the heart of project governance: what does the governance approach seek to achieve? Is it there to blame and castigate individuals for mistakes, or to help the project team achieve project objectives? If, where mistakes are made or risks emerge, a scapegoat is sought, no one will want to be accountable for their actions. This puts the whole project at risk. However, if people feel they are working in an organisation that allows mistakes to be made 'safely', then people will accept their accountability for their actions and immediate responses will be made. This 'psychological safety' is important and requires two key things. The first is an environment that supports and defers to project expertise. The second is a culture that empowers individuals and sets boundaries within which they can act – one which incentivises them to respond to problems rather than just pass them along.

Isolation

Just as we tend to look at problems in isolation from the wider picture, we tend also to do this with responses. Responses are defined to match particular risks and uncertainties. However, individual responses can have wider implications beyond the prevention and mitigation of isolated risks. We respond and then move on to the next problem, not necessarily making linkages between them, or appreciating that containment may well trigger new risks and uncertainties, not only for our own project but possibly beyond it as well. Isolated responses, although sensible, can have unintended consequences that we cannot possibly foresee. Recognising this may not change many of our choices but appreciating possible knock-on effects may widen our sensitivity to the potential ramifications of our decisions and cause us to think more broadly.

Non-commitment

For many project managers, risk is fiction until it materialises. Why act on a fiction if all that does is close off opportunities to act? They may well know about the possibility of particular risks but resist commitment, hoping that the risk will not materialise, possibly until it is too late. Project managers cling to inaction for two reasons. First, they seek to retain their freedom to act. Second, they seek to avoid commitment of resources which may not be needed. Indeed, when budgets are tight, expenditure on seemingly 'non-essential' activities might lead to awkward questions, so this logic has some rational basis. Managers believe these risks might happen, but hope they will not. Some rely on the fiction not becoming reality and therefore refuse to commit – what has been called the 'lure of non-commitment' [1].

Lack of Reflection

We all like to believe that our decisions are well-founded and that we have identified the most effective solutions. However, responses can often be initiated without recourse to detailed analysis to identify whether the chosen response actually matches the problem at hand and to ensure that our judgement is as good as it could be. This automatism is fuelled by the lack of time for useful reflection. Signs of stress and a full workload are good indicators of a lack of reflection in matching a response to a problem and this is worth looking out for in both ourselves and our teams.

Key Enablers to the Art of Containing

One thing that is certain about risk and uncertainty is that they are likely to emerge at some point during a project! We described different ways in which risk can emerge in Chapter 1 (either gradual or sudden). Risk and uncertainty can take many forms and often threaten to derail projects in terms of both timescale and budget and they can jeopardise the realisation of long-term benefits.

Commitment

Beyond investment in creating a group of multi-skilled project workers, other, less financially-intensive activities can be undertaken to develop and ensure a commitment to resilience. However, many of these are predicated on having in place a highly skilled, multi-talented staff.

As we have mentioned, project resilience does not preclude the usual project management processes such as planning, change control, contractual arrangements and so forth. In fact, a crucial part of developing a commitment to resilience is to ensure that all traditional, everyday project processes are continuously improved. Smooth, well-planned processes pay off when adversity strikes. And, should adversity in the form of risk and uncertainty materialise, it should, as far as possible, be tackled within normal project systems and processes – project staff should try to stick with what works on a daily, routine basis. It is only when the everyday processes use up their 'stretch' (as all systems eventually do) that a 'Plan B' needs to be instituted. These times are opportunities for great leadership both to know when to invoke something out of the ordinary and to ensure that morale does not sink as confusion sets in. Ensuring team commitment is not just an act of leadership in the moment though; it needs to be built up over time so that the project or organisational culture is one of dedication to the work and personal commitment to project objectives. This is neither straightforward nor without cost but, when potential crises are successfully averted, this effort will seem like a price well worth paying.

Abundant Expertise

Expertise is not to be confused with 'experts'. Expertise (proficiency, skill, specialist knowledge) is not a permanent state of being but is situational, based on current needs and previous experiences. Expertise is also relational in that it is an assemblage of knowledge, experience, learning and intuition that is seldom embodied in just a single individual.

An expert is often defined as someone very knowledgeable in a particular area. Expertise is unlikely to be defined by hierarchy, status or ego. Nor is it necessarily asserted through accreditations, as these can be just forms of knowledge-testing. 'True' expertise combines deep factual knowledge in a particular field and a way of appreciating that it is dynamic. There is rarely only 'one best way' of doing things in a complex situation and solutions and choices are likely to evolve over time. The expert's opinion is not to be mistaken for the end of a discussion about an answer. Instead, expertise is the beginning of a discourse, triggering a process of fact-finding, knowledge-generation and problem-solving.

The Big Picture

Any response based on expertise not only has an immediate impact on the problem – hopefully for the better – but may have consequences for other problems and solutions. Just imagine that you have responded to a potential risk through taking actions to reduce the likelihood of its occurrence or to mitigate its impact. This is generally a positive process since risks are being actively addressed, as they should be. However, it is important also to keep in mind the impact on the wider project. You may have just allocated resources to solving this problem that were already 'busy' dealing with other problems. The 'big picture' goes beyond the problem and solution at hand. It looks beyond the task or even the project boundaries and incorporates a wider perspective; that of a programme or even a business in which the project is embedded. Management not only involves looking 'down' into the risk or problem, but also 'up and out' to see how this difficulty might interact with and impact on other work. A big picture approach looks at the wider impact of decisions and needs a broad appreciation of goals, priorities and work methods if it is to be able to make sensible judgements in the light of the effects your decisions may have.

Improvisation

In resilient projects, staff understand the importance of routines and procedures for predictable behaviour in delivering the work, but they also know that no one person has complete, perfect, knowledge of the technologies and people systems in and around the project. The unexpected is inevitable. With these surprises (risks and uncertainties) comes the necessity to improvise – the need for staff to think on their feet. Knowledgeable project teams need to have the freedom and space to self-organise into *ad hoc* networks to provide expert problem-solving. These networks have no formal status and dissolve as soon as a crisis is over.

BEST PRACTICE

Spontaneity through Improvisation

A key issue driving the culture within TTP is project type:

> We earn our keep operating at the frontier of new products and new technologies.

The process of creating new technology is a fundamental because:

> That's what turns the engineers and scientists on … creating something that didn't exist before. The 'interesting' bit is important: it's interesting, challenging …

Being at the forefront of technology has the dual benefit of providing interest and engagement for employees while sometimes enabling the company to spot new business opportunities. This is because, within TTP, there is an awareness that the insights gained from creating new products and technologies can also lead to ideas for new businesses. TTP has created new groups and formed several spin-off companies as such opportunities were identified:

> The instrumentation business we've got started out as a contract to develop an instrument. The team developed specialist instrumentation and now offers it as a service in certain laboratory markets.

In exploring, adapting to clients' needs and spotting new opportunities, management has found that:

> One of the key messages that we have here is to be prepared to improvise.

Project managers in TTP face challenges that require new, spontaneous, responses. This is because, at times where planning and execution converge, quick actions are necessary. The work that is required in an environment of pressure and uncertainty becomes less 'formalised' and more improvisational:

> People generally have an instinct to try to do things 'properly'; you see it in corporate strategy and things like that where 'here's the target' – I know our big clients do this – 'here's the target, how do we marshal everything to get there?' Actually, in a creative entrepreneurial environment – and you can do it if you are a smaller organisation – it's more about what are the opportunities, what's in front of us and how do we improvise from that? Darwin, actually as well as the adaptability thing, mentioned improvisation in terms of successful species. It is a central topic and I think it's one that's missed in general, not just risk but in business generally.

Key to improvisational working is, first and foremost, an acknowledgement that improvisation is not a sign of 'bad planning'. Indeed, improvisation works best in a culture in which processes and plans can be circumvented, albeit with set boundaries. Such deviations from 'planned activities' are supported at TTP. Scrutiny is not limited by compliance thinking. Improvisational capabilities are not fostered by compliance audits! Instead, the power of improvisation is measured by its creativity and adaptability. The question of consistency of action is replaced by the question of whether the 'right' action has been carried out in a timely fashion.

Going hand-in-hand with empowerment (letting go), improvisation (making do) leads to increased creative outcomes that are novel and yet at times appear not to be useful. The outcome of improvisational activities might actually lead to otherwise 'wasteful' activities such as 'near-misses'. However in the culture of TTP, such near-misses are seen as opportunities – opportunities to learn.

Improvisation can be prepared for. TTP does not just leave its project managers to 'do their own thing'. Improvisational capabilities are pre-established through training. Again, it is important to point out that compliance to management frameworks – what one should do – is not high on TTP's training agenda. Rather, the aim is to provide project managers with an understanding of what empowerment and improvisation entails – what one can do – in order to deal with situations that are characterised by urgency and uncertainty.

Improvisation is a powerful skill that adds to resilience. It can be developed in members of staff but also needs to be supported by an organisational culture of trust, respect and mutual support. Improvisational skills enable an organisation to be prepared for those risks that are truly unexpected and that require swift action.

Clearly, the resilient project organisation must have some specific capabilities in order to be able to improvise around and outside routines and to form *ad hoc* specialist teams, centred on emerging risks. How an organisation might develop these capabilities is something we discuss later.

WHAT THE LITERATURE SAYS ABOUT ...

Improvisation

Organisational theorists have shown great interest in the ability of managers to be creative and to innovate – in the form of improvisation. Improvisation in organisations is seen as important for making meaningful decisions in situations which require action in a timeframe shorter than the regular planning cycle and/or where there is no predefined course of action [e.g. 2–5]. Various metaphors have been used to provide orientation about what this really entails and the concept of improvisation has been dominated by an ever growing literature on – jazz.

Jazz is rooted in the United States of America. This specific type of music is partly planned yet allows spontaneity. Jazz follows a specific tune, for example. However, within the tolerances of a tune, musicians are 'free' to use their own interpretations in response to other musicians' interpretations. They must, though, still be consistent with and aligned to the original piece.

Improvisation does not come out of thin air. The basic foundation of a jazz piece is a tune or a melody, and these are pre-composed. Yet, the key to improvising is to abandon the shackles of 'order' and create a constant state of creativity and innovation:

> The activity [of jazz improvisation] is much like creative thinking in language, in which the routine process is largely devoted to rethinking. By ruminating over formerly held ideas, isolating particular aspects, examining their relationships to the features of other ideas, and, perhaps, struggling to extend ideas in modest steps and refine them, thinkers typically have the sense of delving more deeply into the possibilities of their ideas. There are, of course, also the rarer moments when they experience discoveries as unexpected flashes of insight and revelation. [6, p. 216]

For non-jazz settings, Weick [7, p. 552] provides a list of characteristics of teams that are required to be highly capable of improvising:

1. Willingness to forego planning and rehearsing in favour of acting in real time.
2. Well-developed understanding of internal resources and the materials that are at hand.
3. Proficiency without blueprints and diagnosis.
4. Ability to identify or agree on minimal structures for embellishing.
5. Openness to reassembly of and departures from routines.
6. Possession of a rich and meaningful set of themes, fragments, or phrases on which to draw for ongoing lines of action.
7. Predisposition to recognise the partial relevance of previous experience to present novelty.
8. High confidence in the team's skill to deal with non-routine events.
9. The availability of associates similarly committed to and competent at impromptu making do.
10. Skill in paying attention to the performance of others and building on it in order to keep the interaction going and to set up interesting possibilities for one another.
11. Ability to match and maintain the pace and tempo at which others are extemporising.
12. Focus on coordination here and now without being distracted by memories or anticipation.
13. Preference for and comfort with process rather than structure, which makes it easier to work with ongoing development, restructuring, and realisation of outcomes, and easier to postpone the question, 'what will it have amounted to?'

Freedom to Think

Improvisation is not carried out in a vacuum. Any action, as novel as it might be, needs to be synchronous – as in a jazz band – with the 'tunes' of other players, namely the other stakeholders. Thinking about how and why one should respond is paramount, but requires time. Such time is often scarce. People tend to be preoccupied with the 'how' – doing things according to what has been pre-planned – and less so with reflection on responses.

Leading the Art of Containing

People experiencing risk and uncertainty need to take appropriate action. Where time is sufficient to prevent a crisis from happening, leadership is required to support the containment of risk and uncertainty. It is tempting to pre-load responses and make people do what has been defined in advance. Uncertainty makes such an approach in itself risky, as novelty and ambiguity require reflection and deliberation, not necessarily the 'blind', almost 'unthinking' adherence to what has been defined as a response to a past problem.

Increasing Readiness

Preparation is just part of the story, though. The preparation of the project team and key stakeholders means that they have the organisational system and understanding in place to scan for and communicate risk and uncertainty and that they are not complacent about their preparedness. However, readiness implies that the team is set to put its preparation into action, to be willing to execute what one has prepared for.

Such commitment to act immediately – when adversity strikes – requires a number of other factors. Key among these is transparency. People must be encouraged not to conceal or hide problems and the outcomes of projects should be measured using an agreed methodology. Apart from anything else, public reporting of outcomes can act as a powerful driver for improvement.

It is also crucial to link staff and worker behaviour to desired outcomes. If organisations want staff to be committed to resilience, they need to be rewarded for this kind of behaviour. This might include the following:

- Bonuses can be linked to behaviour-based expectations (BBEs). Originally used in the nuclear power industry, BBEs are typically agreed among employee peers and they hold each other accountable for seeing that they are fulfilled. They are designed to tackle some common causes of failure, such as lack of attention to detail, lack of critical thinking on the part of staff, noncompliance with policies and high-risk behaviours in high-risk situations. They generally involve ensuring that simple tasks are performed accurately every time, perhaps by developing mnemonics (for checklists) when people are performing repetitive tasks.
- Ensuring that individual owners are clearly identified for all actions, rather than having responses owned by the team. This way, actions are more likely to be implemented.
- Where expected behaviours are exhibited, advancement opportunities are made available.

Facilitating Improvisation

Improvisation can take on a purposeful, considered dimension. A commitment to resilience in projects requires an expectation that project teams will improvise around unexpected problems. In this context, improvisation is not a complete absence of structure in decision-making, implying chaos, randomness and disorder. It is not simply 'making it up as you go along'. Using jazz as a metaphor, the performers (project staff) improvise around a structure and plan. Like jazz musicians, improvising managers continuously invent novel responses without a predetermined script and with little certainty as to the exact outcomes of their actions. The consequences of their decisions unfold as the activities themselves are enacted.

Key to this process is an activity termed 'provocative competence', where managers instigate a departure from routines and 'recipe' behaviour, treating errors as a source of learning. They can alternate between 'soloing' and 'supporting' in order to give the team room to think, enhance learning and distribute the leadership task. There are five steps to provocative competence:

1.   The affirmative move, where the manager has an excellent knowledge of the team's capabilities, often understanding individual team members' strengths better than they do themselves.
2.   Introduction of a small disruption to the routine, such as shifting a regular meeting to a different location or time, or switching personnel around.
3.   Giving the team a problem (or problems) to solve.
4.   Facilitating incremental reorientation by encouraging repetition. This involves learning new routines or ways of doing things based on the problems they have solved.
5.   'Analogic sharpening' – the provocative competence intervention should have allowed the team to work out new links and connections which they can employ in problem-solving. This might, for example, be new or better understanding of others' skills, or new knowledge about resources that they could call upon when faced with a crisis.

Slowing Down Progress

Any response exercised in a project needs to be reflected upon, as the problem at hand might have changed in the meantime. However, a project leader also needs to keep project momentum going in order to meet the inevitably tight deadlines. Managers need to create space for themselves, to think about the 'why'. Why did we do this? What was the purpose of this response and has it had the desired effect? These are just some of the questions that need to be addressed repeatedly. Private, personal reflection is powerful and short daily meetings can also be used to gain greater insight. A suggested balance between 'doing' and 'reflecting' is 90/10. Given the intensity of most projects, this is likely to be challenging. However, it is a powerful approach since it is foolish to believe that a future will actually unfold exactly as planned. Time spent slowing down and thinking is likely to be time well spent.

Deferring to Expertise

As mentioned before, improvisation is not chaos. It is a state of highly situated thinking, dealing with problems in the here-and-now. Such thinking in a collective – as a project normally is – requires expertise both to challenge and also to supplement one another. The hierarchies of traditional, stable project teams can be too inflexible and slow to see and respond to risk and uncertainty in a prompt and effective manner. By the time 'permission' to act has been escalated up the hierarchy to the project leader/director (or possibly beyond to senior, board level management) the problem associated with the risk is likely already to have spun out of control. This is because there is, understandably, a premium placed on progress in projects. The project schedule is one of the key objectives of the work and progress is frequently valued as a key priority. The idea of stopping the project is an anathema to many managers. However, where a problem is identified early, work could be paused briefly to deal with the problem, or risk event, effectively before it becomes much more significant. Caught early, the issue is likely to be relatively small in scope and scale and isolated to a particular part of the project system. The team has to deal with it in a focused manner and then it can move on.

This, then, brings us to a key principle for containing adversity in resilient projects – deference to expertise. Resilient projects push decision-making 'down and around'. Those who are close to risk and uncertainty are often best-placed to deal with the problem. They should not be 'left on their own' to make the best decisions, though. As we have already observed, people in resilient projects are empowered beyond their expertise. However, they must be supported with expertise around them, to enable them to make the most informed judgement.

BEST PRACTICE

Tiger Teams

In Intel development projects, unexpected problems occasionally require some form of trouble-shooting. At the centre of initiating a problem-solving process are so-called 'Tiger Teams' – *ad hoc* small groups of subject matter experts coming together to deal with routine, everyday, problem-solving (and also crises). These Tiger Teams are often 'self-selected', with experts from within and outside the domain in which the project resides. Availability is driven by interest to engage with a challenging problem. The length of engagement is initially estimated, but there is flexibility in extending the time the experts belong to the team until the problem is solved:

> *A Tiger Team would be something where you bring together a set of people for a short period of time to fix an issue. For example, it could be a system that's in production already, but it's gone wrong, or where you've got multiple users and the system has gone down. Or it could be an area within the project that needs special attention and you want to bring in people maybe outside of the project team where you need additional skill sets to help get over the key challenge that's facing you right now ...*

Setting up a Tiger team for a limited period of time requires flexibility in the organisation to provide expertise on an *ad hoc* basis. This is because critical problems are generally not planned for, they emerge. Cost-centred thinking about lending resources to deal with a temporary problem is not a constraint at Intel. As we were told:

> No it doesn't really come down to money, it's more of a priority thing. We're quite flexible so if you want something, send an email or book a meeting with somebody: anyone can talk to anybody so there is no kind of hierarchy in that way. We're an open company in terms of approaching people and looking for help.

Another factor to consider is uncertainty in how long a Tiger Team is likely to be deployed. Without having certainty about when the problem will be solved, stakeholders and cost centres need to be informed and they also need to show time flexibility, allowing their scarce resources to be engaged with the problem until they are no longer needed:

> ... you'd set out a goal to start with to come back in a week's time and have a status review. Generally, in a Tiger Team, you might be sending emails every day about what's happening so people are aware of the progress you're making: to your stakeholders if there's a business impact; and to the resource managers so they understand the progress. After a period of time you'll get to a point where you've resolved it or you understand the issue and then the recommendation comes out of that.

Overall, Tiger Teams are not just a collection of experts, they are experts driven by a purpose or problem statement. Tiger Teams are defined for the purpose of initiating an open and honest struggle to understand multidisciplinary problems by reconciling different perspectives and allowing holistic thinking. Nevertheless, a compromise needs to be struck, with certain trade-offs – about cost and time – which will be discussed and elaborated.

A well-functioning Tiger Team exhibits the following characteristics:

- Openness, trust and respect: everyone is encouraged to speak freely from his or her disciplinary perspective. An opinion is neither right nor wrong; all opinions are respected.
- Common Goal: the goal is to get the problem resolved, and the common goal of trouble-shooting a multi-disciplinary problem is prioritised.
- Commitment: although Tiger Teams are a temporary form of troubleshooting, every expert shows a desire to contribute to problem-solving.

Resilient projects have mastered the ability to alter their typical patterns of containing adversity – they allow the situated voices to be heard. In practice, for resilient project organisations, this means:

- All project workers are valued and expertise is seen as an asset.
- Everyone must be comfortable sharing information and concerns with anyone at any time.
- Project managers defer to the person with the most knowledge of the issue at hand.
- Everyone works together to find the best solution.

The project leader's role is not to be that single expert or to assume that those close to risk and uncertainty have all the necessary expertise that comes with empowerment. Expertise needs to be identified, and made accessible. People need to be made aware of pockets of expertise and how to access them, without great bureaucratic hurdles. A simple phone call to an expert should suffice. Leaders need to encourage a culture in which expertise is acknowledged, cherished and rewarded.

This can take many forms. For example, morning briefings can reinforce deference to expertise using conversational methods, such as non-verbal cues (eye contact, gestures), making problems immediate to people's situations rather than repeating redundant information, and the use of engaging descriptions and storytelling techniques. Whatever method (or mix of methods) is used, it should be rich, current and relevant to the needs of the project workers at that moment. The key is to provoke a conversation around expertise beyond 'surface' information and to spread this knowledge through the interpersonal – and often informal – networks involved in the project. Developing deference to expertise is less about training and more about changing processes. The first step is to redefine meetings. The best place for conversations between leaders and staff is in the work area – not in conference rooms or formal meetings. Project organisations can adopt 'no-meeting time zones' so managers can circulate around the project space and receive feedback from employees, supervisors and other staff members. By observing progress and meeting with employees in their actual work space, leaders can more easily defer to employees' expertise and customs.

Dealing with the Accountability Problem

One issue raised by the deference to expertise aspect of resilience in projects is that of accountability. When projects operate in a resilient manner, compliance should be ensured without resorting to surveillance, since members of the organisation are intrinsically motivated to work with a focus on error-detection and problem identification. Problems are 'owned' by the person closest to them until they can either resolve them or find someone else who can. In resilient projects, problem-based decisions should be taken by those best placed to do so. The challenge in this is that people who experience a great deal of accountability tend to make more accurate decisions but, sometimes, intense accountability can only be relieved by ratcheting decisions up the organisational hierarchy. This is more likely in circumstances where political pressure and career concerns are high. Such examples are the antithesis of resilience in projects.

Supporting 'Wrong' Containment

The principles underpinning responsiveness in resilient projects raise a number of issues. Perhaps the most profound is that of culture. A resilient project needs a culture that supports the behaviours demanded of the project team. Resilient projects are imbued with what is called a 'just' culture. The key focus of this kind of cultural milieu is to concentrate on what is wrong (with the system) rather than on who is at fault. This therefore relies on systems thinking among project teams and project workers. This is absolutely crucial as, for a project to be resilient, every failure, weakness and near-miss MUST be identified. Even one small signal of a risk that is missed could ultimately threaten to derail the project. If people in the project think they will be blamed for the problem, or that the default response will be to identify a person or group that is at fault, then the early, weak signals will go unreported and resilience will slacken. The types of problem and appropriate responses can be seen below (see Table 6.1):

Table 6.1   Just behaviour [8]

Mechanism of duty breach	Appropriate response
Human error: this is an inadvertent slip, lapse, or mistake.	Console the individual. Improve and failure-proof the system that allowed the breach.
At-risk behaviour: this is a conscious drift from resilient behaviour, occurring when an individual believes that drift doesn't cause harm.	Assess the system for weaknesses that encourage or require the individual to take risks. Improve and failure-proof the system that allowed the breach. Coach the individual on the risk taken. Take disciplinary action on repeated risky behaviour.
Reckless behaviour: the individual consciously chooses to engage in behaviour that has unjustified and substantial risk.	Determine if the individual is impaired or unwilling to follow standard work principles. Discipline or provide employee assistance as appropriate.

Another feature of this kind of culture is that it supports people caught up in systemically faulty projects. However, there always has to be balance. Accountability is also valuable and, while room is made for individual failure, if reckless or negligent actions lead to problems these also have to be managed. Finally, and perhaps crucially, a just culture emphasises mutual respect. Behaviours supporting the maintenance of resilience in projects are appreciated, recognised and rewarded.

BEST PRACTICE

A 'Just' Culture

At TTP, there is a need to learn from errors and mistakes. Mishaps, close calls and process upsets are sources from which one can draw lessons:

> We expect that people will make mistakes ... the task of the more senior guys is to manage the consequences of a junior making mistakes. If you're not allowed to make any mistakes, sooner or later you will, and they'll be big ones.

Dealing with mistakes, though, is a delicate issue, as that can always be seen as an acknowledgement of failure, and thus incompetence. Why did the project manager not do the right thing in the first place? It is therefore tempting to ignore mistakes and not share them with others. However, only a small proportion of errors are the result of incompetence or malicious behaviour – something that might justify some sort of blame and penalty. TTP takes active steps to avoid a 'culture of blame' which would undermine the emphasis on teams. There is

> ... very little blame internally ... the people who stay awake all night worrying, they will beat themselves up, they do not need to have somebody else telling them that they have done a bad job.

The lack of a blame culture also means that mistakes can be identified and dealt with early on, rather than being ignored:

> We are communicating to the client ... we have realised something and it was unforeseen ... if it is something where we have made a mistake, we will flag that.

Although everything is done to avoid a blame culture, this does not mean that criticism is frowned upon. Critical and tough questions are expected in group meetings and people understand that the aim is not to attribute guilt but to attain the conditions of a 'just' culture:

It's ok to ask questions, provided you're polite.

A 'just' culture is not to be mistaken for a 'no-blame' culture, which is neither feasible nor desirable. A blanket amnesty, the core of a 'no-blame' culture, without any sanctions, opens the floodgates for unacceptable behaviour. Instead, a 'just' culture provides the encouragement to project leaders at TTP to report and share 'honest' mistakes with internal and external stakeholders. This allows a quick resolution but also facilitates information exchange as a prerequisite for reflection and learning.

Understandably, people are reluctant to share incidents that are burdened with the connotation of failure. As a consequence, TTP emphasises two main issues – confidentiality and fairness. Incidents of errors are communicated without the allocation of blame, and people are incentivised, and occasionally rewarded, for speaking honestly about mistakes and errors in projects they were responsible for. Sanctions for unacceptable behaviours are openly communicated so that people can draw a line against what 'just' implies. It is of great importance that people at TTP are treated fairly. Hence the response to an incident is often explained and justified, to allow people to understand the 'why', without bias and the feeling of injustice.

Supporting a just culture, and acting as a bedrock for the capabilities required for resilient behaviour in projects, are education, training, tools and support. What this involves is 'hardwiring' the behaviours in all project members so that they become natural. Management cannot necessarily change people's expectations. They do not always have the answers about what needs to change – it is the people doing the work that have many of those answers. In order to make sense of expectations and give them life, BBEs have been developed by some resilient organisations. These are where frontline workers meet to come to an agreement on what expectations they would hold each other accountable for. What these are is specific to the individual project – it is for the project leader to help groups synthesise clear expectations that makes sense within the context of the work. However, it is important that they tackle the routine issues that the project workers face every day and turn these from routines into expectations, thereby significantly reducing their potential to generate risk. For example, on a construction site, everyone might be expected to wear a hardhat. This is reinforced by notices, fines, exclusion from the construction site for anyone seen not wearing a hardhat, and so on. Just as it is now the norm for nearly all car drivers to wear a seatbelt, so too does it become a *cultural* norm, continually reinforced, that all construction workers wear a hardhat at all times when they are on site. Anyone not wearing a hardhat is regarded as odd, an outsider, not of 'this culture'.

WHAT THE LITERATURE SAYS ABOUT ...
Culture and Sensemaking

Culture has been explored by anthropologists and sociologists for decades and, perhaps inevitably, attention has turned to smaller societal units, namely organisations. Much of the literature concerning organisational culture is rooted in the wider literature of anthropology and sociology and much of the terminology is borrowed from those disciplines. Thus, when thinking about organisational culture, the discourse is oriented around belief systems, values, symbols and customs.

Trying to pin culture down to a single, meaningful definition was always difficult but two American anthropologists, Kroeber and Kluckhohn [9, p. 181] categorised and summarised numerous definitions to arrive at what has become generally agreed to be a useful starting point. They define culture as:

patterns, explicit and implicit, of ... behaviour acquired and transmitted by symbols, constituting the distinctive achievements of human groups, including their embodiment in artefacts; the essential core of culture consists of traditional ... ideas and especially their attached values; culture systems may, on the one hand, be considered as products of action, on the other, as conditional elements of future action.

Broadly, this definition underpins most of the characterisations of organisational culture which focus on the collective expectations, experiences, philosophy and values that bind the members of the organisation together. These are based on the shared attitudes, beliefs, customs, and written and unwritten rules that have been developed over time within the organisation and are considered valid by its members.

An amusing illustration of the difficulty in pinning down what organisational culture really means comes from the American leadership guru, Ellen Wallach, who observed *'organization culture is like pornography; it is hard to define, but you know it when you see it!'* [cited in 10, p. 193].

Culture is notoriously difficult to analyse as values are intangible and can only be inferred from the manifest symbols projected by the organisation and the behaviour of its members (see Figure 6.1). However, there are a number of ways of making sense of organisational culture. Perhaps the most well-known means of characterising culture in organisations is to think of it as layers, with the observable artefacts and symbols at the periphery, with values and then underlying basic assumptions residing inside them [11, p. 11].

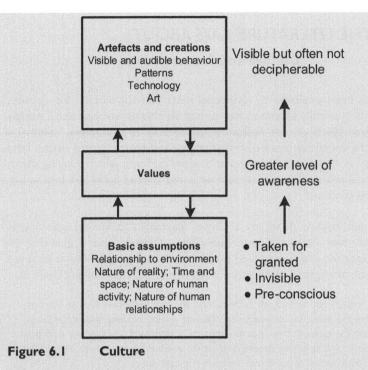

Figure 6.1   Culture

The question might be meaningfully asked as to why we would want to examine organisational culture at all. The reasons are that culture impacts on the way members of the organisation behave in profound ways [12, p. 164]:

- the ways the organisation conducts its business, treats its employees, customers, and the wider community,
- the extent to which freedom is allowed in decision-making, developing new ideas, and personal expression,
- how power and information flow through its hierarchy,
- how committed employees are towards collective objectives.

Given the strong influence of culture on the way organisations behave – not only for the purpose of containing adversity – culture has important implications for resilience in projects. Perhaps paradoxically, then, it may be surprising to discover that among the first things we can learn from resilient organisations is that we should not try to tackle the culture – at least, not directly. Management cannot readily change the culture. It can provide the slack for people to come together to ask 'what prevented us from getting the feedback we needed immediately?' or 'what kept us from being resilient when things went wrong?' but they do not have the answers. The answers must come from the frontline workers and they can discover them only when they are able to be in conversation about things that matter. It is conversations that change the culture. So changing culture in organisations becomes:

- not tackling 'culture' but tackling specific problems,
- using sensemaking to find the problems and understand the norms related to those problems,
- accepting that management cannot easily change the expectations that people hold of each other.

To look at these points in turn, Schein [13, p. 189] noted that managers should

> never start with the idea of changing culture. Always start with the issue the organization faces; only when those business issues are clear should you ask yourself whether the culture aids or hinders resolving the issues.

Sensemaking, in the context of culture, is broader than a meeting to look at a specific issue. It is about how the organisation constantly and vigilantly uses the knowledge embedded in people's minds to learn what has gone wrong and what to do about it. Sensemaking meetings may have many different labels and take many different forms. Sensemaking can become a part of any staff meeting or gathering. What is required to move the culture is to bring together people who pick up on the weak signals or who have experienced near misses or an event. This can be used to understand what is going on in the organisation. Some examples of ways in which sensemaking might be enacted include:

- impromptu 'huddles',
- *ad hoc* networks,
- more formal problem-solving meetings,
- 'lessons-learnt' debriefings,
- interdisciplinary task forces,
- formal staff meetings.

Whatever form these sensemaking meetings take, they have some common aspects which project leaders need to encourage if they are to shift culture and uncover the norms and expectations that reduce reliability:

- inclusion of frontline staff,
- creation of appropriate space,
- development of a tone of curiosity and learning,
- promotion of interaction among members,
- skilful facilitation.

Supporting Purposeful Containment

As we mentioned earlier, in a resilient organisation the person who responds first to a problem because they are closest to it and thus most familiar with it is generally to be supported. However, in drawing on his or her specific expertise, the individual may look at the problem in isolation from the larger view of what that problem could mean for the project and the wider business.

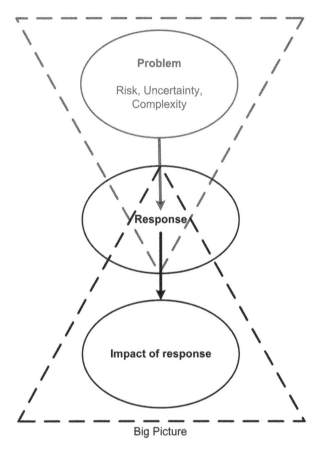

Big Picture

Figure 6.2   Big picture thinking – solution

A project leader may well execute a response without thinking about the potential consequences of it on the big picture (see Figure 6.2).

The project leader needs to make sure that the first-responder is sensitive to what that big picture includes and challenge them to make the connection between their response and its possible wider consequences. The simple question 'What does this mean for … ?' may actually suffice to kick-start this consequential thinking. Widening someone's appreciation will also influence their ownership. Something that, looked at in isolation, may appear to be relatively inconsequential, might suddenly become more important if seen in the context of the bigger picture.

Project leaders need to have a good oversight and be aware of the wider implications of risk responses, rather than becoming embroiled in the detail. Yes, they are formally project managers but, in their leadership role, getting involved in day-to-day issues may divert attention from the broader, system-wide issues. Keeping sight of the 'big picture' means that they will be able to help the project team form and maintain a shared sense of the adversities it faces and the appropriate actions to take. Ways in which project leaders can communicate this wider understanding include telling rich stories about how people have identified and tackled risks and uncertainties in previous projects and how this has led to the delivery of all the project objectives. Encouraging everyone to communicate openly with each other, especially in situations that seem odd, unusual, or problematic, is powerful. Finally, crucial to communicating the 'big picture' are formal, coordinated, briefings which act as a means of giving people a common framework in advance of their work activities. In these briefings, discussion can centre on the assumptions they hold about what they will face, how they are going to function and how they are going to update their mental pictures about what is going on.

The Impact of Containing on Relationships

Suppliers and subcontractors are frequently used for many types of project and one of the biggest challenges for projects with aspirations of resilience is the involvement of the supply chain in the process. The question facing project managers is: 'how do we engage with these organisations who may have little or no interest in doing anything differently?' The challenge is that, where suppliers and contractors are responsible for aspects of the project delivery, their involvement is crucial if the project team is to be able to respond effectively to the early, weak, signals of risk events. There are a number of strategies that can be employed to help make this happen.

Assessing Contribution

The first task for the project manager or director is to assess the actual contribution of suppliers and contractors to the project. Ideally, this will be in value terms. So, what proportion of the project delivery is being undertaken by your suppliers and contractors? (Note: this can be financial or strategic value. One supplier may be providing a relatively inexpensive but customised component that is central to your new product's functionality. This should be considered as an important contribution if its failure could derail the whole project.)

If suppliers and contractors have a large input into project delivery, particularly with people involved in critical project work, then the first strategy is to determine the relative importance of each supplier or contractor to the project. Here it might be useful to employ a simple Pareto analysis. Essentially, this involves establishing roughly which 20 per cent of suppliers and contractors are contributing approximately 80 per cent to the value of the project. It is in these high-value activities that risks are likely to have the largest impact on the overall project. Consequently, it is these suppliers and contractors who are the top priority for engagement in the precepts of resilience and response.

Driving Commitment of Suppliers

How can you engage them? This has to be on the same basis that you engage project staff and workers within your own organisation, but the crucial difference is that the supplier organisations need to operate within a structure that allows this engagement to happen. Traditional contracts and specifications are often insufficient. These key suppliers and contractors have to mesh with the procuring organisation through the use of non-traditional, partnering-type contracts. These contracts can ensure early involvement in planning decisions, open-book accounting and novel pain-gain incentives around risk management. More crucially, where employees from suppliers are involved in project work, partnering-type contracts can blur the distinctions around who belongs to which organisation. The goal here is for the project staff and workers to see the project itself as their 'employer', not the organisation who pays their wages. Commitment to resilience in projects means commitment to the project, not commitment to your employing organisation. Success in this is, unsurprisingly, difficult but building strong, trusting, relationships this way can serve as a valuable foundation for future contracts and hence can be beneficial for many years to come.

Addressing the Accountability Problem

We have talked about the importance of accountability and the establishment of a 'just culture' and indeed about the role of culture in supporting accountability and both facilitating and controlling empowerment. This is always going to be problematic if one dominant organisation seeks to impose its culture on all members of the project team. Therefore, it is incumbent on the project manager/director, to see that the project develops its own organisational culture. This will clearly overlap with the culture of the parent organisation but should be somewhat distinct – a set of values and belief systems that is unique to the project.

An additional difficulty with implementing this is the often transient nature of suppliers in projects. Frequently, suppliers and contractors will be employed to, perhaps, complete a specific work package or activity. This means that their staff or workers will enter the project, do their work and leave. This can, indeed, be a continuing phenomenon in projects, with people and organisations coming and going throughout the project lifecycle, especially for 'transactional' tasks. One way of tackling this additional problem is to decide well in advance of the project's commencement which suppliers and contractors are crucial to project delivery and to engage them in the process even as part of their tendering arrangements.

The main risk with this approach is the exclusion of the 80 percent of suppliers and contractors whose contribution represents only 20 per cent of its value. Although they may not be responsible for a substantial contribution, they may be crucial in other ways. For example, a specific supplier might be responsible for a key activity on the critical path, where that activity itself is of little overall value to the project. A delay to the critical path is a threat to the overall delivery of the project, so these organisations also have to be fully engaged with the tenets of project resilience. We have already mentioned that expertise can be seen as being a function of interrelationships among team members and that team expertise is usually greater than that of the individual. Therefore, where suppliers and contractors contribute crucial components to the team these individuals also need to be brought into the project partnering arrangements.

Never-ending Containment

It must be acknowledged that containing adversity is an ongoing process and not a one-off activity. Adversity in the form of risk and uncertainty constantly jeopardises project performance. By no means can adversity be fully prevented from materialising. Indeed, it can only be subdued to the extent that variation in project performance may remain within acceptable tolerances. Hence, all the parties involved need to acknowledge that the initial 'ideal' of project performance may never be achieved.

Towards an Art of Containing

We often assume an inherent desire to respond to something 'new' that has not (yet) had a tangible impact on project performance – risk and uncertainty. Even though we might enact a response, and probably overestimate its positive impact, we may still rely heavily on past experience rather than thinking about how this novel problem requires a novel solution.

A resilient project requires dedication and a desire to respond. Such a desire can only be realised if project members are empowered and skilled beyond their 'silo' of allocated responsibility and accountability, in order to deal with novelty and abnormality. In this respect, the escalation of decisions up the organisational hierarchy for the purpose of receiving greater authority to enact a response indicates a lack of such empowerment.

Empowerment is a crucial component of achieving a commitment to resilience, the confidence to improvise and the ability of project organisations to harness the latent expertise within project teams. This expertise can be valuable when directed to dealing with risk events in the here-and-now. However, empowerment does not mean that project managers/leaders give up control, as this would be a risk in and of itself. The question becomes one of how project managers protect their projects from control failures when empowered employees are encouraged to redefine how they go about doing their jobs, improvising and acting autonomously.

Equipping people with range flexibility may allow forms of improvisation. This, though, is not to be mistaken for an acknowledgement of bad planning, since improvisation is a key skill in a project team. However, it can only be applied successfully if the 'big picture' is established and maintained. Responses exercised in isolation of their wider impact are simply a 'shot from the hip' and are potentially dangerous.

It is unsurprising that project leaders need to support 'first-responders' in a project, but they should resist the temptation to take over. It is the project leader's task not to be bogged down in day-to-day work but to provide a support network that allows people closer to the problems to deal with them in a timely and appropriate fashion.

Reflection

How well do the following statements characterise your project? For each item, select one box only that best reflects your conclusion.

	Fully agree		**Neither agree nor disagree**		**Fully disagree**
People are committed to engaging with risk and uncertainty.	1	2	3	4	5
Ambiguity in predicting the future is not a hindrance to creating practical responses to it.	1	2	3	4	5
People are empowered beyond their immediate responsibility.	1	2	3	4	5
	Fully agree		**Neither agree nor disagree**		**Fully disagree**
Training and expertise is provided to allow people to deal with abnormal situations.	1	2	3	4	5
The 'big picture' is maintained or established by project leaders to allow 'first-responders' to appreciate the impact of their responses.	1	2	3	4	5
Hierarchical escalations are an indicator of a lack of empowerment.	1	2	3	4	5
	Fully agree		**Neither agree nor disagree**		**Fully disagree**
Expertise is valued more highly than hierarchy, status and position.	1	2	3	4	5
Project leaders help and support in facilitating a response; yet they do not take over if something goes wrong.	1	2	3	4	5
Unless grossly negligent, people are not penalised for enacting a 'wrong' response.	1	2	3	4	5

Scoring: Add the numbers. If you score higher than 27, your capability to prepare for uncertainty and complexity would appear to be good. If you score 27 or lower, please think of how you may be able to enhance your capability to respond to risk appropriately and in a timely manner.

References

1.   Kutsch, E., T.R. Browning and M. Hall, Bridging the Risk Gap: The Failure of Risk Management in Information Systems Projects. *Research-Technology Management*, 2014. 57(2): p. 26–32.

2.   Crossan, M.M., Improvisation in Action. *Organisation Science*, 1998. 9(5): p. 593–9.

3.   Crossan, M.M., R.E. White, H.W. Lane and L. Klus, The Improvising Organisation: Where Planning Meets Opportunity. *Organizational Dynamics*, 1996. Spring: p. 20–35.

4.   Miner, A.S., Organizational Improvisation and Learning: A Field Study. *Administrative Science Quarterly*, 2001. 46: p. 304–37.

5.   Weick, K.E., Improvisation as a Mindset for Organisational Analysis. *Organisation Science*, 1998. 9(5): p. 543–55.

6.   Berliner, P., *Thinking in Jazz: The Infinite Art of Improvisation*. 1994, Chicago: University of Chicago.

7.   Weick, K.E., Improvisation as a Mindset for Organizational Analysis. *Organization Science*, 1998. 9(5): p. 543–55.

8.   Marx, D., *Whack-a-Mole: The Price We Pay for Expecting Perfection*. 2009, Plano, Texas: By Your Side Studios.

9.   Kroeber, A.L. and C. Kluckhohn, *Culture: A Critical Review of Concepts and Definitions*. 1952, Cambridge, Mass: Peabody Museum of Archaeology and Ethnology.

10. Knox, D.L. and S.S. Butzel, *Life Work Transitions.com: Putting Your Spirit Online*. 2000, Woburn, MA: Butterworth-Heinemann.

11. Schein, E., *Organizational Culture and Leadership*. third edn. 2004, San Francisco, CA: Jossey-Bass.

12. Whitman, M. and H. Mattord, *Management of Information Security*. 2013, Boston, MA: Cengage Learning.

13. Schein, E., *The Corporate Survival Guide*. second edn. 1999, San Francisco: Jossey-Bass.

Chapter 7

THE ART OF RECOVERING

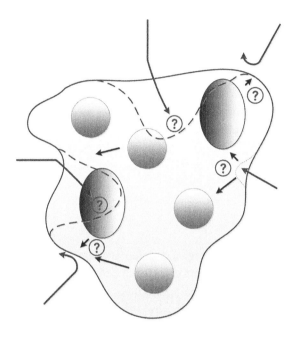

You may not have been able to prevent all risks and uncertainties from influencing your project. The preceding normality has cascaded into a crisis situation in which your project's continuation is threatened. Unsurprisingly, this is a time of considerable stress. Yet, it is a time in which clarity is required and poorly thought-through actions need to be avoided. With emotions being stretched to the limit, objectivity is of the utmost importance to enable an appropriate recovery.

The Lure of a 'Great Escape'

Imagine that all that has been written in the previous chapters has not worked out. Risk, uncertainty and complexity have taken their toll and if no actions are taken – swiftly – the project might be suspended or stopped altogether. With so much at stake, what do you do? When a crisis hits a project, there are often specific types of behaviours, similar to the ones described in the previous chapters and yet considerably amplified. These too are counterproductive because, ironically, they can reinforce the chaos instead of helping with a solution.

The Defensive Retreat

In a crisis situation characterised by chaos, one is likely to lose orientation. 'Where are we?', 'What is happening?', 'What shall we do (quickly)?' are some of the questions that project staff ask themselves in their new situation. As a result, and because of that uncomfortable feeling of 'being lost', we often tend to fall back on our basic instincts – on self-preservation. We become more inward looking and try to cover ourselves as individuals. Divisions that emerged during the incubation time (if there was any) may intensify. Instead of more collaboration, we shift towards more adversarial relationships. We start building a wall around us that gives us an illusion of comfort. Collaborative decision-making becomes less likely.

Broken Communication

Going hand-in-hand with increased defensiveness in the face of a crisis is a change in the way we communicate. Communication can be used to preserve our integrity and even to damage others. Information is exchanged, not necessarily for the purpose of exploring what is happening or what we should do next but to lessen any potential blame attaching to oneself. Emails sent for the purpose of explaining one's decisions and leaving a trail to be used later to justify one's actions make sense in that narrow personal context, but may not help the project in the here-and-now. Communication can degenerate into accusations and thus becomes more destructive than helpful in crisis recovery. It is especially important to look for this in inter-departmental or client-provider communication as each group may well retreat to its own domain for relative safety if it looks as if the project is unravelling. When trust falters, resorting to 'formal' communication alone can virtually eliminate the spontaneity, collaboration and improvisation that may be vital for a resolution at that moment.

Centralising Power

Perhaps you are in the midst of a project crisis but have avoided building a defensive wall around you, retrenching and resorting to a blame game. There is a tendency, when we do not see progress from others, to feel the need to assume control. We believe that we can do better, and that by transferring power to ourselves we can single-handedly deal with the situation more effectively than we could as a group. Unfortunately, this form of centralisation (and the accompanying power games) is often a side-effect of a crisis situation in projects.

Thinking and Acting in the Past

It is likely that this crisis, in its totality, is of a type that you have not directly experienced before. However, human nature means that it is also likely that you will rely on recovery mechanisms you have deployed in the past. Tackling a novel problem that requires quick and decisive action through drawing on past solutions is not only likely to be ineffective, but might actually exacerbate the crisis. We are habitual creatures and we tend to rely on our past experiences and schemas of action. However, these past-informed habits may not fit the present crisis. Being aware of this may enable you to focus more clearly on new, more creative, solutions to the current problems.

Tunnel Vision

Under increased stress, the scope of our radar narrows and shortens. Our minds tend to focus on single actions, and the insufficiency of a response in alleviating the situation is compensated by further fixation on executing it, sometimes over and over. Such fixation may prevent us from remaining sensitive to the bigger picture of what is going on around us.

Key Enablers to Recovering

The behaviours that typically emerge in crisis situations are ones that need to be actively managed. Usually, the goals when faced with a crisis are its immediate resolution and 'damage control'. This is important, but so too is a necessary shift in the way the crisis is managed. As quickly as possible, the recovery stage needs to be initiated.

Project Continuity

This book is very much about the 'soft' aspects of project management, about behaviours and applied practice. Nevertheless, one cannot ignore the need for some structure. Every crisis response involves business continuity planning. For project work, this continuity plan defines which functions in the project it is critical to address and maintain. For example, in a software development project, a critical function might be the 'testing environment' in which sections of code are brought together and functionally evaluated. If these critical functions come to a standstill, the whole project could be put on hold. In a crisis, such functions deserve special attention. So, a plan is important in that it helps to be ready. What it does not do is prepare a project team for a potential crisis.

Checklists

In a crisis, the resulting stress and 'tunnel vision' may actually be countered by the relative 'automation' of a checklist. A checklist should not replace human situated cognition, but it can help to probe the situation and aid a project manager's mindfulness. A good checklist is one that is:

- Short and simple. Simplicity forces project managers to accept a stimulus, and to interpret.
- Focussed. It aims at critical functions of a project. Insignificant components of a project are not checklisted.
- Practical. It only offers probes based on actions that are doable and feasible.

Closeness

We might have all the necessary plans in place but because of the unfamiliar character of a crisis, people are not ready to exercise those plans, let alone be reflective and creative. The question this raises is how to sensitise people for a crisis, in a safe environment, before the crisis actually happens. One answer lies in simulating worst case scenarios. Crisis simulations have the great benefit of getting close to risk and uncertainty situations. Playing and living through worst-case settings, to test ones endurance and adaptability in a 'live' but safe environment, is at the core of simulating crises.

It is a great puzzle that, in many projects where substantial value is at stake, planning and preparation involve tools and techniques that do not really incorporate the emotive side of managing risk and uncertainty. Most planning approaches advocated in project management seem to exclude the behavioural side of a crisis. If you can, simulate a crisis that allows you to receive immediate feedback on key stakeholders' behaviours and skills under high-stress conditions. It is too late to test these out when a real crisis is already unfolding.

WHAT THE LITERATURE SAYS ABOUT ...

Threat-rigidity

A large body of literature focuses on the inability to alter responses in the face of change – so-called 'threat rigidity'. This research has focussed at multiple levels, addressing effects on individuals, groups and organisations [e.g. 1, 2, 3].

At an individual level, threats are often related to the level of stress and the corresponding inclination to trigger dominant habitual responses, encouraging a rigid response that may not match the changing circumstances. Alongside stress, anxiety may lead to a narrowing of perception. In times where more cues need to be processed, anxiety tends to lead to decreased sensitivity. Performance appears to be increased only in cases where the central cues are picked up by the individual and the execution of well-rehearsed responses does actually help the problem at hand.

Threats to groups may have the temporary effect of generating greater cohesion, yet, if the threats continue to jeopardise performance, adverse effects are observed. The initial challenge of the situation brings people together. Nevertheless, continual challenge does not automatically increase cohesion in the long-term. In order to maintain group cohesion, some – if only short-lived – perception of successfully overcoming threats is fundamental. Yet, those most influential in the initial phases of a threat tend to lose some of their control and power. There are only a few – exceptional – cases in which leaders actually strengthen their influence under these circumstances.

Finally, at an organisational level, threat-rigidity is linked with the increase in formalisation and standardisation, and in the enforcement of procedures. This increase in the pursuit of control goes hand-in-hand with the centralisation of power, a well-acknowledged side effect of facing a major threat. The number of decision-makers is generally reduced. Overall, organisations seem to enhance control in times of perceived chaos by imposing greater rigidity on structure and practices.

Threat rigidity is not just a proposition or a theory but something that is likely to constrain the ability of an organisation to adapt to novel threats.

Tiger Teams

When a crisis strikes, seeking an outsider's perspective can be vital. Internal politics tend to take over in the middle of a major problem as people can become insensitive and defensive and may entrench themselves in their silos.

If one wishes to find a swift solution to avert disaster, this silo mentality needs be broken up. Tiger Teams (whether they are called that or go by some other name) can deliberately be set up – high-performing teams aiming to reconcile potentially opposing views and facilitating solution-finding in out-of-control situations.

They need to be on stand-by or hovering around a project, monitoring the situation and ready to provide the project manager with support. They can be parachuted in when the situation warrants it. A Tiger Team does not necessarily replace the project manager but focusses on the following:

- listening and asking questions from multiple perspectives about what is happening and yet not rushing to conclusions despite the pressure to act quickly.
- imagining worst-case implications together with the details of complex, potentially dynamically-changing, tasks.
- suppressing members' own egos in terms of 'knowing the answer' yet remaining inquisitive in creating options.
- willingness to break existing rules and processes, with the ability to think outside of the usual methods of operation.
- skills to create solutions that work at the technical, process and human levels.
- ability to maintain a continuously-high level of focus and intensity of action.
- maintaining all this to achieve rapid project recovery while operating within challenging timeframes under the 'spotlight' of senior management.

In projects, the role of the project manager is frequently an 'everything' function. They are often expected to switch seamlessly from managing 'business as usual' to being a crisis manager. The shift from normality to a crisis-like situation however, can be difficult for managers who are emotionally and structurally attached to the project. Instead, a set of seasoned managers, possibly currently involved in other projects but with scope to provide the necessary support to a project in trouble, can be used to provide that valuable input. Members of the Project Management Office (PMO) can also form part or all of a Tiger Team if the organisational structure supports that.

It is surprising to note that Tiger Teams have not found their way into project management standards. Indeed, project management frameworks do not seem to acknowledge that a crisis actually falls within the realm of project management. As alien as a crisis in a project may be, the approach should not be 'if' it happens, but 'when', and Tiger Teams are known to be effective and valuable in breaking down silos and overcoming entrenched positions.

However, the formation of a suitable response team can be difficult. This can especially be the case within organisations where silos exist which may hamper the process of developing trust and *ad hoc* cross-functional networks. This can be particularly so where the project team comprises members from different organisations, adding the significant extra complication of contractual and other transactional barriers. This can, though, be addressed in a number of ways. Foremost, for any team to be successful it must be given clear objectives and goals. This is especially important for an *ad hoc* team and the project leader has the responsibility of keeping the team focused on the goal of resolving the problem that has emerged. Secondly, given the pressure and visibility it will be under, an *ad hoc* team needs the clear support of senior management. It needs to be given the necessary freedom, but with sufficient time and the relevant resources to enable a successful outcome. The challenge is often exacerbated when members of *ad hoc* teams are given this new responsibility while also being expected to continue in their existing roles. This lack of prioritisation is often inappropriate. It may be more suitable to pause the troubled project when the problem is identified and seek to resolve it using additional expert resources before allowing the *ad hoc* team to disband and its members to return to their day-to-day activities.

A leader of an *ad hoc* team generally has less authority than a 'standard' project manager and can offer fewer rewards. This makes managing more difficult and influencing and motivation skills are vital. Rewarding and recognising team members is important and resilient projects and organisations will find incentives that encourage and reward teamwork. Appraisal and reward systems are often centred on individual performance rather than team outcomes, so it is important to emphasise and reward being a team player. Interpersonal relationships can be central to success, so managers also need to ensure that they foster key team relationships as best they can under such demanding conditions.

Logistical Independence

The resources that have been provided for project 'normality' may not be the most suitable to help in a crisis situation. Indeed, one may argue that the resources deployed in the incubation phase of a crisis have been insufficient to prevent it from occurring in the first place. The Tiger Team has to draw on a pool of readily or quickly made available resources, be it people or additional funds. This access to resources should be detached from the daily business of the project. Lengthy, otherwise sensible, change-related processes need to be unhooked or circumvented.

Nevertheless, this does not imply that the provision and deployment of resources for the purpose of stemming a crisis should be allowed to unfold in a haphazard fashion. Similarly, the question of how this extra resource is paid for should not add to the difficulties of the project. Preparations should ideally be made in advance of any crisis occurring. Arrangements may, for example, include the provision of a budget for these resources (as yet unspecified, since the nature of any future crisis is unknown) in advance of their mobilisation. As we encounter time-consuming 'blame-games' in crises, the risk of silo-mentality associated with lengthy and often futile searches for root causes could be overcome by switching to a contractual model that 'shares' the costs of managing a crisis, regardless of which party 'caused' it. This focuses minds on solutions, not blame.

Sustained Commitment

Very similar to value-driven risk management (see Chapter 3) in which 'value' takes centre stage, rather than the risk attached to it, commitment to the purposeful management of a crisis is of paramount importance. At times when defensive retreats encourage a focus on one's own 'survival', commitment to one's silo and commitment to old versions of the management of 'normality', a crisis requires the definition of a new, clear and compelling vision. People do not just let go of routines that have worked in the past. A new commitment towards recovery needs to be prepared for and rapidly deployed in order to facilitate the switch to crisis mode.

Leading the Art of Recovering

A crisis in a project is often perceived as threatening, a period of confusion which requires urgent remedy. It is at these moments that project managers need to be 'leaders' as their staff will look to them to 'do something'. The challenge for leaders in projects is to 'bring things back to normal'.

Readiness to initiate a radical shift in the mode of management is required in advance – from a phase characterised by shock, confrontation and increased response rigidity, to one of reflection, collaboration, and adaptation. Leadership is required to prepare stakeholders for such a necessary transition and to facilitate a move from potential inaction and rigidity towards recovery.

Readying Stakeholders

A crisis needs to be prepared for. Stakeholders need to be educated for 'when' it happens, not 'if'. Of course, if at all possible we want to prevent a crisis from ever happening and this is the focus of all the planning that goes into projects. The result of this effort is an unspoken assumption that failure will not (cannot) happen, and this makes readying stakeholders for engaging with a crisis all the more difficult. Doing so is an implicit acknowledgement of failure. It also costs time and effort to prepare stakeholders for a crisis in the absence of one. Why prepare for something that has not happened yet and may not happen anyway? This is a valid question and needs to be addressed by leaders and by project managers. A project manager has to allow time and effort, often in advance of the execution of the project, for techniques that allow key stakeholders (for example, the client) to rehearse a crisis, and to test the response capability to deal with one. Whether such rehearsing involves the development of plans, simulations of scenarios, or simply storytelling, does not matter, as long as the approach helps to sensitise people to the emotive factors of a crisis. Words in isolation, in the form of a plan – dry, impersonal – are inadequate to convey the behavioural side of a crisis.

Being Reluctant to Press the Panic Button

Project leaders need to set expectations in circumstances where people look to them for guidance. The temptation is to convey messages that the situation is likely to turn out for the best. On one hand, this optimistic perspective instils confidence and motivates, but it might also lead to positive illusions of control and thus to blind spots. If people absorb the confidence that everything will go well, they may become less vigilant, and less adaptive in their understanding. The result may be greater rigidity and inaction in response to the unfolding situation.

On the other hand, portraying a doomsday scenario encourages fatalistic behaviour, in which people sit back and let fate play its cards. It is down to the leader to find an appropriate balance in setting expectations – between being too optimistic and pessimistic. Generally, we tend to underestimate the severity of a crisis and overestimate our capabilities to deal with one, so a project manager should tend to look at challenging over-optimism.

Being Hesitant to Centralise

Defensive retreats often go hand-in-hand with the urge to centralise. Leaders may lose trust in other people because they did not prevent the crisis from happening in the first place. As a result, leaders may be tempted to rein in many tasks they have previously delegated. Be warned! If you do this, you may find it difficult to focus on what a leader is supposed to do in a crisis – facilitate an understanding of the problem and its solution. Being bogged down in detail prevents you from maintaining sensitivity to what is happening. Help people not to take anything for granted and drive situational awareness by asking questions that surface new and important knowledge.

A crisis requires courageous action, yet it is not up to the leader to take all the courageous actions. Indeed, leaders need to let go and facilitate action where it matters, close to the problem, and develop the commitment to respond in the most sensible and valuable way. Such commitment cannot be taken for granted, given that people may retreat into their shells and may exhibit rigidity, only responding to cover themselves. Such self-preservation in times of upheaval is common (and understandable) and needs to be addressed by project leaders. This commitment should be supported by the provision of a wide response repository for those 'firefighters'. Extensive power needs to be channelled down to front line staff, while leaders remain sensitive to what is going on and intervene if necessary. A premature intervention may be interpreted as a sign of distrust or simply suggest that power is centralised and does not require any response from those closest to the problem.

BEST PRACTICE

Supporting the Resolution of Bigger Issues

With bigger issues at hand that require a quick resolution, existing project resources are unlikely to cope with the pressure to act. Information overload, so common in crisis-like situations, is the result. At Intel, the project team is supported by a Management Review Committee (MRC), not dissimilar to a Steering Committee. As was explained to us:

... we always have an MRC review body. This is where you have senior management support to help address those issues that you're facing. Whether it's a resourcing issue, a budgetary issue, a timelines and expectations issue, there is continuous communication with your management review committee.

An MRC consists of cross-functional expertise and seniority:

... it will be various levels of management in that business team's management chain as well as the IT team's management chain. So, if you're working for Marketing on a very, very important project you might have the CMO [Chief Marketing Officer] involved. If it's important to a certain section of Marketing it might be a GM [General Manager] or Director from that business. So, the MRC is quite a broad organisation but the layers will depend on the scope and the criticality of the project on the business side. Then you'll have the relevant IT resource managers involved so that they can help augment resources and remove road blocks from an IT execution standpoint.

However, a Steering Committee often focuses on:

- providing 'authority' to the project team and helping to govern the distribution and migration of authority;
- representing stakeholders;
- ensuring that decisions meet the needs and wants of stakeholders;
- acting as ultimate decision-makers.

This rather traditional view of a Steering Committee is one of centralised decision-making, in which wisdom and power carry more weight than the one closest to the problem – the project leader. At Intel, the purpose of the MRC is not just to make decisions. Decisions or support for recommendations by the project team are a key function of the MRC but it also ensures that the project is continually aligned to overall business objectives as these can change to smaller or larger degrees through the lifetime of the project.

It is more aligned to collective ownership from an agile standpoint. It's not like 'that's your role' or 'that's your role, you're to blame', it's all about the collective ownership of the team to come together to work out the options. So, when you're going to the MRC you're bringing options. 'These are the things that we think we can go and do to resolve.' We are not saying 'here's an issue without any sort of recommendation to it.' The MRC isn't going to solve it for you!

The role of the MRC is therefore to:

- maintain a perspective of collective ownership;
- make decisions based on recommendations from the project team;
- continually align the project to business objectives;
- create options for the project rather than imposing solutions;
- help to remove road blocks on the way to a problem solution;
- challenge the project team's thinking by offering alternative perspectives.

The advantage of this kind of Steering Committee, the MRC in the case of Intel, is that it provides benefits that go beyond the 'traditional' role of a Steering Committee. It is seen as a 'forum' where views and ideas are exchanged first, to help a project team without questioning team commitment or competence:

> I think, if there's a project viability issue, then one of the recommendations you make coming out of the project is 'we don't think this is viable anymore', but it's not for the project team to make a decision just about the project, the business needs to be supportive of that direction. We need to support that direction and understand why you're making that recommendation and then again ask difficult questions. For example, did it align with that? Did they see opportunities that we're missing? We understand the problem statements, explore the initiatives, explore the decision process and then ultimately make a decision.
>
> It probably also acts as a good forum if you've got a project with a fairly widespread stakeholder map where you've got people who are coming from very different business groups that are coming together and benefiting from the value of your project. Here, the MRC acts as a good forum to bring those together and almost 'level the playing field' a little bit. They act as a place where everyone can hear the different inputs that the project team are having to deal with and the thought process that goes through and the recommendations that come out of that forum.

Maintaining Trust

A crisis can be deliberately triggered because of hidden agendas. Crises encourage people to be more defensive and walls are consequently built around silos – defensive retreats. In this situation, trust can evaporate. Trust can be established (or re-established) by project managers who focus on showing compassion and concern. In a crisis, people may think that their own work and importance is diminished. If, for example, a Tiger Team has been parachuted in to mediate, other stakeholders may find themselves side-lined. Show 'real' concern to each and every project team member. Consider the necessity of shifting power, for example, to Tiger Teams and address and explain the rationale for the decisions that have been made.

Showing concern goes hand-in-hand with being honest and transparent. Communicate that there are conflicting perspectives and expectations; be honest about the pressure that people are under but show optimism that solutions are feasible. Provide pertinent information in 'real-time'. Outdated information may be misinterpreted as following a hidden agenda.

However, although communication in a crisis is essential, it needs to be controlled. Unreliable information may only add to rumours and fuel false impressions. People want to air their opinions, especially when their own positions and departments are involved. Unwarranted speculations about what is happening or what might be done are detrimental if project managers fail to control them. Offer your project members valid information and plenty of opportunities to voice their opinions, but information (or a lack thereof) should not be turned into ammunition to serve political agendas. Facilitate communication in an open and honest manner by assuring the reliability of its content.

Manage Behaviour, not Plans

Crisis management plans or checklists – outlining sets of predefined, 'mechanistically' performed actions – are there for a reason, to provide some form of structure and order in an environment perceived as being chaotic. However, these plans can be a double-edged sword. On the positive side, they help to trigger behaviours quickly and efficiently. Conversely, they may suppress situated human cognition. If plans do not adequately match the situation at hand, people may blindly walk into disaster. Project leaders need constantly to reflect on the appropriateness of plans and their execution. If a plan does not appear to match the situation as they perceive it, the project leader must deviate from it. Ultimately, you manage behaviour and plans are there to support this, not vice versa.

Channel Resources to Where they are Needed First

Contingency plans do help to pinpoint critical functions in a project. The question of 'What must not go further wrong?' – a question often not asked – drives a greater understanding of the most vital resource allocation. In a crisis, one may tend to throw resources at anything that poses a threat. A much more effective course of action is to prioritise the deployment of resources to where they actually matter. For example, if we talk about a project that delivers a range of benefits (e.g. functions), then systematically categorising what must or should not go wrong (any further) is a sensible approach. The 'must not' requires greatest attention and forces a clear prioritisation.

Learning from Crises

A crisis, in which a project stands at the edge of disaster, requires reflection and learning. However, we often want to detach ourselves from this uncomfortable experience. The urge to forget and move on to other tasks can leave the potential for learning untapped. Learning from a crisis, if it happens, often takes the form of analysing, documenting and allocating root causes, with the purpose of standardising responses to any future crisis. In its own way this appears to be a sensible solution, unless we operate in an environment in which crises unfold in random patterns. However, expecting a similar crisis to hit you another time may, in itself, form a root cause for future failure.

Learning should go beyond the past, and learners – project leaders and project participants – should be reluctant to replace valuable human cognition with yet another additional layer of prescribed process and procedure without a strong rationale for doing so. But how? Storytelling is considered a very powerful mechanism to convey rich context – an event or crisis – and provide a platform for the 'listeners' to develop their own learning.

A 'good' story:

- is authentic and one which the 'listener' is familiar with and can relate to;
- combines words with images and audio to appeal to all our senses;
- is connected to an organisational narrative or a bridge is built so that the story is linked to the context of the listener;
- provides a clear structure, often helped by a timeline;
- is simple and relatively short, so as to maintain attention.

People naturally make sense of experience through storytelling and therefore it can be a very powerful learning tool. Storytelling done well can encourage reflection, inspire current and future collaborative approaches, stimulate enquiry and help to build knowledge and understanding. Additionally, cultural and emotional contexts can be understood and acknowledged as being important. It is only one way to reflect upon practice and find ways of making sense of crises but, compared with dry, codified knowledge that may never be read, it is a very accessible means of learning. Indeed, it happens anyway. In social gatherings, project managers trade 'war stories' of what went wrong in projects they have been involved in. Storytelling takes this out of the informal, social context and gives it a more formal and structured role in organisational discourse.

BEST PRACTICE

Challenging Ways of Working

In The Technology Partnership (TTP), it is the responsibility of project managers to explore beyond the 'known expertise'. They do this through extensive empowerment but this only works if access to additional know-how is provided:

If you need particular expertise on a project you can pull it from anywhere in the company.

The provision of additional expertise gives project managers multiple perspectives but does not constitute a delegation of responsibility. Deference to expertise, as exercised at TTP, is aimed at:

- seeing your project from a different perspective;
- encouraging scepticism;
- acknowledging adversarial views;
- challenging your own assumptions.

All of this is done in the interest of making fewer assumptions, noticing more and ignoring less. This is really all about addressing risk blindness – the ability to notice blind spots – and is carried out at TTP using an elaborate process of 'peer-reviews':

We have a peer group review system. There will be monthly project reviews where a peer or peers will review with the project leaders ... to assist the project leader to stand back and think 'Well I want to do it that way but ...

This process acts as a 'sensor' to highlight blind spots and, in TTP, is carried out by independent functions:

When we do a technical review, we normally invite someone who is not involved directly on the project because they can come and often spot things that someone who is too close to it cannot see.

TTP's peer-reviews are not designed to 'check' whether project managers are compliant with the organisation's rules and procedures. Instead, they are designed to make project managers think about what they are doing and, most importantly, why:

It is to stand back and think about what you are doing.

They will ask you difficult questions and spot things that you might not have thought of yourself.

You start to recognise some early signs [of failure].

Even in times of urgency, where there might be a temptation to rely on an 'autopilot' mentality and just replicate what one has been doing in the past, deference to expertise provides a 'sanity-check':

> It's taking a step back to try and see whether you are doing the right thing.

The implementation of such a peer-review system has its challenges, too. Project managers might see it as 'big brother', watching over them and telling them what is right and what is wrong. Or, they might rely on the peers as a crutch to help them make decisions rather than making decisions for themselves. This is why challenging assumptions, with the aim of detecting risk blindness, should not include the imposition of 'answers', it should only help the one who owns the project – the project manager – to create answers. In TTP, the peer-reviewing mechanism acknowledges the 'folly of imposed solutions' and offers support to make a project manager think and be creative in his or her problem-solving – it is NOT about making the project manager obey. This is in stark contrast with many other organisations, where 'auditing' is used to ensure that employees remain within a supposedly self-evidently correct management framework. Not so TTP, which uses expertise 'just' to inform.

WHAT THE LITERATURE SAYS ABOUT ...

Learning and the Importance of Reflection

Learning has attracted the attention of a large number of researchers. Across different bodies of literature, the aspect of learning has been researched from individual to organisational levels [e.g. 4–8]. Much of the literature agrees that learning is not 'just' the creation of knowledge, but something that leads to a change in knowledge, beliefs, behaviours, routines and attitudes. However, a troubling pattern has seemed to emerge in which managers find it very difficult to change their ways of working based on past failures and even more so on past successes.

Individuals, groups and organisations spend considerable effort accumulating knowledge. Meetings are held to share experiences about past or ongoing events, diaries are updated and reports are written which document successes and failures. Even though this captured, codified, knowledge is made available to others, reflecting on and changing in light of such knowledge remains limited and, in many cases, non-existent.

The key to changing 'fixed' knowledge into learning is reflection. The major theoretical roots of reflection lie in the works of John Dewey, Jürgen Habermas, David Kolb, and Donald Schön. For example, Dewey observed that it is not from experience itself that we learn but, rather, reflecting on that experience [9]. The word 'reflection' implies thinking about oneself and, as such, describes a form of experiential learning. It is something we instinctively do as human beings. At an organisational level, the key is to capture and direct this natural process into a form of learning that can benefit the organisation and the communities within it.

Models exist, primarily in the education field, that seek to make sense of and understand how reflective learning occurs. Perhaps most well-known is Kolb's model of experiential learning [10], where reflection is seen as being central to a cyclical process of identification, review, questioning and reconstruction. Here, 'Knowledge is continuously derived from and tested out in the experiences of the learner' [10, p. 27]. Arguably, this is where there is space and time to think back on past events.

Donald Schön [11, p. 21] discusses the importance of storytelling as a mode of reflection:

> ... for storytelling is the mode of description best suited to transformation in new situations of action ... Stories are products of reflection, but we do not usually hold on to them long enough to make them objects of reflection in their own right ...

When we get into the habit of recording our stories, we can look at them again, attending to the meanings we have built into them and attending, as well, to our strategies of narrative description.

Without reflection, learning becomes merely surface activity and is not embedded. Without embedding learning, one is destined to be trapped in what Argyris characterises as 'single-loop' learning – where one becomes an expert in making, and fixing, the same mistakes over and over again. Failures happen and these are blamed on existing processes which are then applied with even more rigour and refinement, creating the same mistakes again. This illustrates the need for reflection (to break the single-loop cycle). Moon [12] outlines the conditions for reflection – time and space, a good facilitator, a supportive institutional environment and an emotionally supportive environment. What is needed are:

- ill-structured, 'messy' or real-life situations;
- asking the 'right' kinds of questions – there are no clear-cut answers;
- setting challenges that can promote reflection;
- tasks that challenge learners to integrate new learning into previous learning;
- tasks that demand the ordering of thoughts;
- tasks that require evaluation.

The Impact of Recovering on Relationships

A crisis is a time of high emotion with the project viability at stake. The threat of stopping or suspending the work and the resulting potential damage to the reputations of all the parties involved hangs like a dark cloud over the heads of stakeholders. It is important that crisis management efforts are not only targeted at the most vulnerable and most critical functions, but also at those people who are most affected (these are not necessarily those in the thick of it). Relationships are at stake.

Establish Clarity in the Key Contact Points

The antithesis of a defensive retreat is to break down barriers and share information freely, while being sure to control the accuracy of the information. Sharing information should be done with the help of clear contact points. Stakeholders should not need to seek out sources of information on crisis updates or how the crisis is being dealt with. An obvious choice is the project manager, who is most often closest to the evolving situation and has the clearest view of events. Yet, he or she may already have their hands full dealing with the operational side of a crisis. Ideally, a key contact point should have objectivity and a 'helicopter view' – like a Tiger Team. In this respect, the Tiger Team should be equipped with skills of facilitation, communication and conflict resolution to serve in the role.

Be Open and Accurate

The single contact point, possibly in the form of a Tiger Team – trusted by all parties involved – should provide timely, frequent and accurate information, and mediate between stakeholders if necessary. In addition, if that contact is someone other than the project manager, that provides some 'breathing space' for those who are preoccupied with 'hands-on' crisis recovery activities.

Listen

An important aspect of crisis management is that of caring through listening. Listening to stakeholders offers them the chance to air their concerns. Listening is not as easy as it may seem, though. Reflective listening involves both content checking and feeling checking. Content checking implies mutual acknowledgement of each other's understanding of what has been said. Restating content provides reassurance of a shared understanding.

Feeling checking is not so much about the content but about the emotions, involving feedback and reflection on each other's emotional state.

As with so many skills that are important in a crisis, listening for the purpose of showing that one cares for another's content and emotions is not without barriers:

- Anticipating a message: you may already think or expect in advance what the person is going to say and hence you might interrupt them.
- Rehearsing an answer: while the person is trying to convey their message, you may already be thinking about an answer and thus you will not give them the attention they deserve.
- Thought wandering: a cue by a person may make your thoughts wander off. This may lead to misinterpretation and the need for that person to repeat the message.
- Premature conclusion: you may already have come up with a conclusion although the message is incomplete.

Collectively Owning a Crisis

A crisis, regardless of whether sudden or creeping, is often caused by a multitude of factors. Hence, searching for a single root cause is often a futile exercise. Not having a root cause in place does not negate the collective 'ownership' of the crisis, though. However, ownership is not to be mistaken for accountability. A project manager may be held accountable for what he or she does to resolve the crisis by providing timely feedback and measuring progress toward recovery. Ownership, though, is the obligation of the collected stakeholders. Ownership is created by establishing collaboration and a sense of partnership in the belief that recovering from a crisis is in the best interest of all parties. Commitment from all parties involved to engage in timely (and often costly) actions of troubleshooting is highly valuable and provides a sense of cohesion.

Think Long-term Relationship

A characteristic of a defensive retreat is myopia – short term thinking. Members of a project tend to ask themselves during a crisis how to recover from it quickly. Their horizon may not move beyond the phase of recovery. However, not only is the project at risk but also the long-term relationships with stakeholders. Questions need to be asked about what happens after a successful recovery, and how (potentially) damaged trust between stakeholders can be re-established. It is dangerous to wait until after the crisis has passed to consider how groups and individuals could and should work together in the longer term. Projects are (by definition) transient and, although it is difficult when current work is in turmoil, it is important to consider future projects and the sustainable working relationships that will be necessary to support them.

Sharing the Burden of Recovery

It is tempting in a crisis to look for a root cause and allocate the burden – costs, emotions, responsibility for recovering from it – to those believed to be the triggering factor for the predicament. This search for single-point failures and single-point accountability is often already manifested in the choice of contract. Projects most often rely on a 'traditional' type of contract, with a focus on the position of one party to the contract in relation to the actions of the other parties. Essentially, this can set up an adversarial relationship, with each party to the contract protecting its own position and looking to maximise its own benefit. The contract itself can encourage and exacerbate the adversarial stance taken by the various parties delivering the project. The focus can shift to personal gain rather than the goals of the project. This is the antithesis of project partnering wherein there is an implicit (and often explicit) assumption that all parties involved in the project are committed to a single goal, while recognising the different and shared needs of the various organisations involved. Perhaps, then, traditional contract forms might be inappropriate. This is well-understood in many project environments and has led to the development of a variety of alternative, more collaborative, contract forms. With collaboration comes the incentive to 'share' the costs of tackling problems. Typical of these types of contracts is some form of shared pain/gain agreement, whereby the costs of failing to meet milestones or objectives are shared among project participants. By the same token, if the objectives are met, the project is delivered efficiently and is handed over below budget or early, then all participants can share in this outcome. The incentives are aligned. The client is able to make use of the delivered project and this frees up any residual budget, some of which can be shared between the organisations actually delivering the project. The key is to encourage swift and efficient collaborative problem-solving while avoiding the sometimes crippling transaction costs that are so often the outcome of more traditional contract forms. These transaction costs have two effects on the project: they can mire the project participants in bickering over where the fault lies, rather than focusing on resolution, and they involve inordinate record-keeping and costly arguments over who is to blame, often resulting in extensive legal disputes long after the work has been completed.

In order to avoid some of these problems, collaborative, partnering-type projects will normally be 'open-book' whereby the client and the project team can view each other's project documents. There are two main justifications for this: organisations have to trust each other and it avoids the need for costly claims. Hidden agendas are (hopefully) removed and the project staff and workers start to focus on the needs of the project rather than those of their organisations. All being well, organisational needs and project needs start to align with each other.

Celebrate a Victory

Overcoming a crisis is a feat to celebrate. Crises do occur and often are not preventable. They are high-pressure situations in which emotions take the upper hand and recovering from one deserves recognition. However, it is tempting to lay the memories of such a painful phase of the life cycle to rest, to forget and to move on. Stakeholders need to recognise their successful recovery and rebuild potentially damaged relationships. By celebrating victory over a crisis, negative connotations about its occurrence can, at least to some extent, be alleviated.

Towards an Art of Recovering

A crisis is something to be anticipated. Risk and uncertainty will sometimes slip through our defences, and complexity will do the rest in creating a state that threatens the viability of a project. This threat increases the pressure for a project leader to act and emotions will run high. Counterproductive behaviour is to be expected and needs to be managed carefully. Defensive retreats need to be broken down and objectivity re-established. Organisational capabilities for dealing with 'normality' are often ill-suited to deal with a crisis. Additional capabilities, for example the use of a Tiger Team, may need to be parachuted in.

The previous sections provided a range of suggestions on how to cope with a crisis in a project. These suggestions – and just to remind the reader, these are just suggestions – are encapsulated in the following statements:

Reflection

How well do the following statements characterise your project? For each item, select one box only that best reflects your conclusion.

	Fully agree	Neither agree nor disagree			Fully disagree
We have a common understanding that crises are a normal, yet infrequent, part of project life.	1	2	3	4	5
A crisis needs to be managed in a methodical manner. We implement generic crisis management plans to deliver robustness and responsiveness. We give priority to a potential/looming crisis and resource a response appropriately.	1	2	3	4	5
We reflect on our behaviour in a crisis in order to learn to deal with future events.	1	2	3	4	5

	Fully agree	Neither agree nor disagree			Fully disagree
We use independent personnel to give objectivity and help develop solutions in crisis situations.	1	2	3	4	5
We accept that decision rigidity may hamper the development of an effective response and we provide appropriate levels of freedom to enable creative solutions to evolve.	1	2	3	4	5
We try to care for every stakeholder by keeping them informed of the evolving situation and addressing their particular needs.	1	2	3	4	5

	Fully agree	Neither agree nor disagree			Fully disagree
We recognise that managing the full flow of information is critically important in a crisis situation. We provide relevant and timely information in a calm, orderly and controlled manner.	1	2	3	4	5
We recognise the importance of unambiguous power and our managers control the balance of power effectively during a crisis.	1	2	3	4	5
We prepare for crises by experiencing them via simulations and do not rely exclusively on a written crisis management plan.	1	2	3	4	5

Scoring: Add the numbers. If you score higher than 27, your capability to prepare for uncertainty and complexity is good. If you score 27 or lower, please consider how you may be able to enhance your capability to successfully recover from a crisis.

References

1. Chattopadhyay, P., W.H. Glick and G.P. Huber, Organizational Actions in Response to Threats and Opportunities. *Academy of Management Journal*, 2001. 44(5): p. 937–55.
2. Hannah, S.T., M. Uhl-Bien, B.J. Avolio and F.L. Cavarretta, A Framework for Examining Leadership in Extreme Contexts. *Leadership Quarterly*, 2009. 20(6): p. 897–919.
3. Staw, B.M., L.E. Sandelands, and J.E. Dutton, Threat-Rigidity Effects in Organizational Behavior: A Multilevel Analysis. *Administrative Science Quarterly*, 1981. 26(4): p. 501–24.
4. Schwab, A. and A.S. Miner, Learning in Hybrid-Project Systems: The Effects of Project Performance on Repeated Collaboration. *Academy of Management Journal*, 2008. 51(6): p. 1117–49.
5. de Holan, P.M. and N. Phillips, Remembrance of Things Past? The Dynamics of Organizational Forgetting. *Management Science*, 2004. 50(11): p. 1603–13.
6. Novak, J.D., *Learning, Creating, and Using Knowledge: Concept Maps as Facilitative Tools in Schools and Corporations*. 1998, New Jersey: Lawrence Erlbaum Associates.
7. Levinthal, D.A. and J.G. March, The Myopia of Learning. *Strategic Management Journal*, 1993. 14: p. 95–112.
8. Argyris, C. and D. Schon, *Organisational Learning: A Theory of Action Perspective*. 1978, New York: Addison-Wesley.
9. Dewey, J., *How We Think*. 1933, Boston: D.C. Heath and Co.
10. Kolb, D.A., *Experiential Learning*. 1984, Englewood Cliffs: Prentice Hall.
11. Schön, D., *Coaching Reflective Teaching*, P. Grimmett and G. Erickson (eds), 1988, Teachers College Press: New York. p. 19–29.
12. Moon, J., *Reflection in Learning and Professional Development*. 1999, London: Kogan Page.

Chapter 8
ROADS TO RESILIENCE

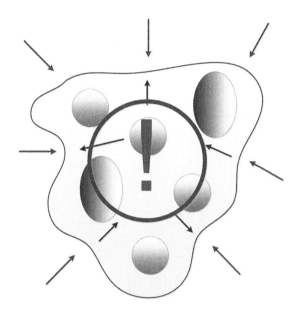

As we have seen, projects are constantly challenged by the effects of risk and uncertainty. Based on experience and having a memory of past events, organisations build up defences which are continually maintained and updated in an attempt to keep risk at bay. At the same time, though, organisations, projects and teams also develop capabilities to adapt to the uncertainties they face. These aspects of resilience can appear contradictory and can sometimes work in opposing directions. In this final section, we will synthesise what has been written about project resilience and offer a way forward while also appreciating how difficult it is to be resilient in the true sense.

A Road Map

The previous chapters provided us with 'lures' that need to be recognised, as they constrain our ability to manage risk, uncertainty and complexity effectively. These lead to leadership principles that work hand-in-hand in our quest to develop resilience, as shown in Figure 8.1.

Resilience

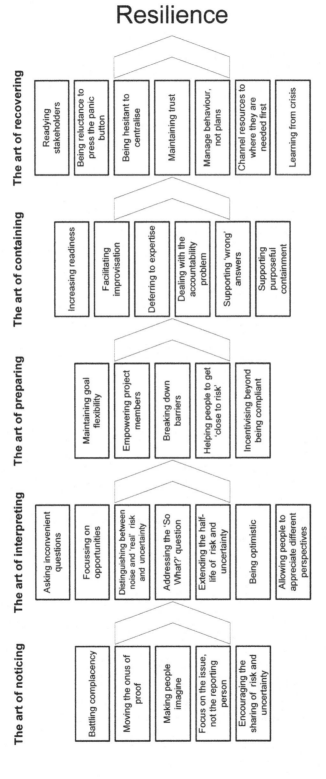

Figure 8.1   A road map towards resilience

It is important to realise that this is not about process. These factors work together to facilitate greater awareness among the project participants, with a view to developing a more resilient culture. Together, these principles enable the team to prepare for the unknown and to respond confidently. It is not possible to eliminate all potential problems, nor to plan with sufficient accuracy so that all eventualities are covered. However, it is entirely feasible to develop the capability to respond more effectively and to prevent issues escalating so rapidly into crises.

These enablers are not 'traditional' in the sense of the compliance systems often promoted as effective in a strongly hierarchically-structured project. Indeed, you are unlikely to find this style of language in many texts focusing on tools and techniques. Our emphasis has been to take the human side into account, to enable and support practical decision-making and address the fallibilities inherent in all of us. These ideas do not, of course, replace the valuable body of material on issues such as planning, resourcing, control and so forth. There are many fine publications that will help managers with these aspects. This book is intended to complement such ideas, not to replace them.

The leadership activities we highlight differ somewhat from the spirit of 'command and control' that some authors advocate. The focus here is not on the accuracy of predictions or compliance with plans, but rather on aiding and allowing the project team to think freely – within boundaries – and supporting timely and appropriate responses to contain uncertainty.

Despite our differences in perspective, our strategic objectives are the same – to:

- provide a greater likelihood of achieving the desired result;
- ensure efficient and best value use of resources;
- satisfy the differing needs of the project's stakeholders [1].

And yet, our road-map towards achieving these commonly accepted benefits of project management may be slightly odd, different to what one would expect. Your road-map, of course, would be very much different to our suggested one. How would it look?

Reflection

The depicted roadmap (see Figure 8.1) is a synthesis, but, yet again, it is devised from the perspectives of the beholders, the authors. Please take a piece of paper and develop your own benefits map, and think about your current project or even a future one.

Step 1: What capabilities do you have in place to realise your project? The capabilities are structural, procedural and behavioural. It is useful to restrict yourself to using only nouns to describe these capabilities.

Step 2: Define changes (as seen in Figure 8.1) to current ways of working. For this, you may articulate these changes as verbs. Make sensible associations between your enablers and changes.

Step 3: Think about what benefits/objectives you will achieve, based on your enablers and changes. Use adverbs and adjectives to articulate those benefits/objectives.

Step 4: Carry out a gap-analysis. Prioritise your benefits/objectives and see whether some changes or enablers need particular attention.

You may want to consider involving only two or three key stakeholders in creating a Project Benefits Map. This joint activity creates understanding and ownership but also challenges one's view of the state of project resilience, for a current project or one in the future.

A Practical Switch

We have advocated the role of mindful capabilities in facilitating positive project outcomes in uncertain environments. However, these need to be balanced with rule-based management, and this leads to potential tension in the application of both. In principle, the two approaches contradict each other, with the application of one seeming to exclude, to some extent, the other (see Figure 8.2).

This can be a challenge for both the project leader and the recipients of project leadership. It may be difficult to reconcile or combine these perspectives and uncomfortable to consider switching between them. From a leadership perspective, organisations and projects commonly start with a predominantly rule-based approach, supported by a transactional leadership style. This (often default) way forward may then be challenged by unexpected events, with a consequent deviation from expectations. Often a crisis is needed to trigger a rethink from a transactional to a transformational style of operating.

However, we can also approach this (as a thought experiment) the other way around. Uncertainty is generally highest at the beginning of a project, when many aspects are unclear, unknown, or even unknowable. In such a situation, transactional leadership may be inappropriate, and a transformational style

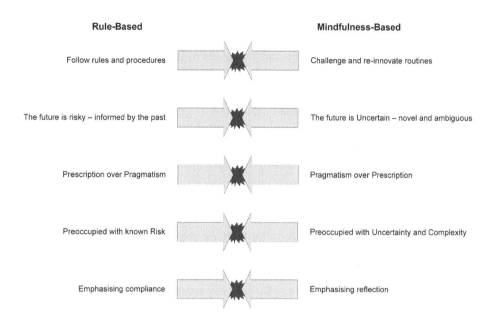

Rule-Based   **Mindfulness-Based**

Follow rules and procedures — Challenge and re-innovate routines

The future is risky – informed by the past — The future is Uncertain – novel and ambiguous

Prescription over Pragmatism — Pragmatism over Prescription

Preoccupied with known Risk — Preoccupied with Uncertainty and Complexity

Emphasising compliance — Emphasising reflection

Figure 8.2   **Conflict between two modes of management**

that emphasises mindful capabilities may be preferable. The closer one moves to the risk horizon or, in other words, the more uncertainty is reduced over time, the greater is the potential need for a practical drift towards to a transactional leadership style. That style can be maintained once the project finally transfers to a business-as-usual state of operation.

At the beginning of projects that contain uncertainty, members should be open to mindful practices. Flexibility and openness can counter knowledge absences within the work and support a pragmatic attitude of 'doing what needs to be done' as the work unfolds. As uncertainty diminishes and the end becomes visible, it makes sense gradually to switch over to a more rule-based approach. For example, a product development project might begin with a range of possible options but by the time the customer launch is planned and the manufacturing and logistics are scheduled with the supply chain the details need to be firm and well-founded.

This gradual switch can be challenging, as it involves a changing ethos over the duration of the work. To counter this difficulty and prepare the team, running a simulation of the project may be valuable. Try bringing your key stakeholders together and – in a safe environment – practice and rehearse how such a practical evolution can be made to happen. This enables all the participants to experience the challenge of doing so in advance of it happening for real, so they can internalise the rationale and anticipate this in the actual project. An understanding needs to be conveyed as to why this gradual change to the ways of working is beneficial, and what the impact of this drift will be for stakeholders. If necessary, contractual changes may have to be made alongside these adaptations. That could imply that one starts off with, perhaps, a pain/gain share agreement (given the uncertainty at the beginning), moving on to a more fixed price arrangement. Although this may be difficult, even discussing it means that the thought processes are underway as part of an ongoing conversation.

Rehearsals and simulations allow ideas to be tested and the results experienced. Although it is satisfying to plan everything on paper, learning by doing provides tangible feedback and a memorable emotional impact that should not be underestimated, despite the cost of running such a simulation. Subsequent resilience can be supported by a mental state that draws on this previous familiarity (albeit fictitious).

How, then, do organisations actually incorporate mindfulness in practice? As part of our research with a range of organisations in the UK (not those named in the case studies), we have identified four response styles, each with their strengths and weaknesses.

Pure Rule-based

There may well be projects out there that are certain. In other words, one can predict and manage risks, and foreknowledge is a sufficient basis for confidence in how the project will unfold. We can expect minimal deviation from the plan, the goals are fixed and will not be challenged by internal or external influences. Stakeholders are predictable, and amenable to the project objectives.

In this rather idealistic environment, the 'traditionally viewed' way of project management can – and should – be applied (see Figure 8.3). The tools and techniques of the profession will serve you well. The underlying premise is that pre-loaded plans and principles will sufficiently accommodate any form of adversity. Management by exception, by relying on situated human cognition, is discouraged. Rule-based management as a pure form of planning and control is the dominant doctrine.

Figure 8.3   Pure rule-based mode of management

This approach to dealing with potential critical incidents offers a stable, transparent – because of pre-loading – environment, in which external resources can be integrated relatively easily, as they only have to comply with a limited set of rules and procedures.

In our research, we have seen such an approach, where organisations set up and use rule-based approaches and discourage deviations from their application. Such preparedness is often, however, challenged by a lack of readiness to deal with problems that were not identified and pre-planned in advance of their occurrence. Particular challenges we observed when issues arose were that if an employee (e.g. an engineer or project manager) could not solve the problem there and then, it escalated through the organisational hierarchy. This could lead to delays and lengthy arguments about the root-cause of incidents, especially in buyer-supplier relationships. This lack of a clear 'ownership' of the problem could result in both a lack of progress and a souring of relationships between parties involved, further exacerbating the situation. Most people can relate to such a situation, which can be attributed – to some extent – to the inadequacy of the applied doctrine of rule-based behaviour. We have observed, though, that this tends not to lead to a change in the way of working, so the scenario may be expected to repeat itself at a later point in time.

In Table 8.1 we distinguish between 'preparedness' (the work done to try and ensure that the organisation is in a state to start the project, with the expectation of a smooth piece of work) and 'readiness', in which we highlight the particular challenges that arise in practice.

The upside of a rule-based approach to managing projects by compliance is one of efficiency. Resources can be deployed as planned, and can be (relatively) easily substituted. In some cases this is a sensible approach, for example where the work is comparatively routine and does not require much deep expertise, but in reality this is uncommon. Most projects are challenging to manage in this way.

Table 8.1   Insights into preparedness and readiness of pure rule-based mode of management

Preparedness	Readiness
Compliance to pre-defined problems and actions. Governance structures, processes and mechanisms prepared and utilised to ensure stability and control.	Solutions to deal with novel problems may require an 'unfreeze' of standards and frameworks.
Stability of rules and procedures. These become known, understood and ingrained within the organisation so that project participants are 'pre-loaded' in terms of how to operate and what will be expected of them.	Required escalations of novel problems may translate into arguments on accountability, hence slowing down the resolution of the problem at hand.
Transparency of decision-making in times of normality. The hierarchy is clear, and the lines of control are well-understood.	
Facilitation of integration of external resources. Minimal reliance on specialist resources so that flexible deployment is feasible.	
Efficient deployment of resources. Pre-planning means that underutilisation of resources should be minimised.	

Reflection

How well do the following statements characterise your project? For each item, select one box only that best reflects your conclusion.

	Not at all	To some extent	To a great extent
People are expected to be compliant with rules and procedures.	1 2	3 4	5
There is little discretion to deal with a risk beyond our rules and procedures.	1 2	3 4	5
We are predominantly incentivised by following rules and procedures.	1 2	3 4	5
There is little time to reflect on how we do, could, and should manage risks.	1 2	3 4	5
Coming up with new ways of working is not encouraged.	1 2	3 4	5

Scoring: Add the numbers. If you score higher than 15, your project provides little room for being mindful in how you deal with uncertainty. Please think whether your approach to managing risk and uncertainty is appropriate for the nature of the work. If you score 15 or lower, your approach to managing a project allows for engaging with risk, and in particular with uncertainty, in a mindful manner.

To reiterate, this book is not about a set of planning processes for the purpose of greater prediction and control. There are numerous standards that cover such frameworks and they do have their benefits. This is about project resilience in a wider sense, to allow people engaged in projects to be mindful; to activate situated human cognition to contain uncertainty. Project resilience is about:

1.   making people *uncomfortable* about uncertainty;
2.   providing the *comfort* of being able to deal with uncertainty beyond what has worked in dealing with risk in the past.

'Just-in-time' Mindfulness

The constraints of a rule-based approach can be alleviated by the provision of mindful capabilities and we have identified several ways in which this can be manifested. The first we labelled the 'just-in time' mode (see Figure 8.4), and this involves the creation of temporary mindful capabilities to deal with an emergent problem until it is resolved. Most often, this happens via the *ad hoc* formation of 'Tiger Teams', consisting of cross-functional experts. Such a team can be formed quickly to enable extra resources to be added at a time of need. This 'new' team, unencumbered by having worked on the project to date, can aid in the resolution of the critical incident. This 'fresh set of eyes' can be beneficial, and can free up the existing project team to run normal operations and ensure that the parallel 'business as usual' aspects go smoothly.

The main difference here is that mindful capabilities are deployed temporarily – just to deal with specific events that have arisen – yet these are not the same resources as before. Additional capacity is 'parachuted-in' for a limited period of time, until a state of normality has been re-established. Meanwhile, the already-deployed resources remain preoccupied with the day-

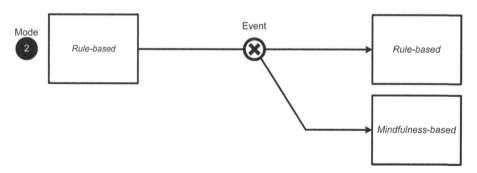

Figure 8.4   **'Just-in-time' mode of management**

**Table 8.2   Insights into preparedness and readiness of 'just-in-time'
mode of management**

Preparedness	Readiness
Compliance with pre-defined problems and actions.	Temporary acceptance of overriding authority to deal with novelty.
Stability of rules and procedures.	Overlapping and, at times, conflicting competencies.
Transparency of decision-making.	Emotional and structural detachment from the Tiger Team in order to solve critical incidents objectively.
Facilitation of integration of external resources.	Delay in deploying mindful capabilities while the new team is assembled.
Efficient deployment of resources.	
Definition of additional mindful capabilities, often in the form of 'Tiger Teams'.	

to-day project activities (see Table 8.2). This is not necessarily straightforward, though. It requires the availability of the additional capacity, and they are unlikely to be on stand-by waiting to be called upon. Hence the organisation's leaders must be ready to prioritise work rapidly and make decisions on resource deployment when necessary. This itself requires a flexible operating approach at the higher management levels.

'Infusion' of Mindfulness

We have also seen a balance of the rule-based and the mindfulness-based approach, whereby those working on the project can change their predominant way of working when unexpected incidents occur. This involves invoking mindful capabilities, though not extra capacity, when pertinent (see Figure 8.5).

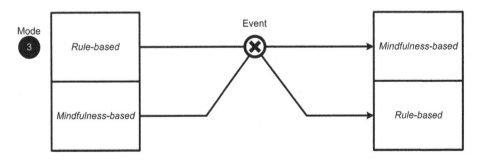

Figure 8.5   'Infusion' mode of management

Table 8.3   Insights into preparedness and readiness of 'infusion' mode of management

Preparedness	Readiness
Compliance with pre-defined problems and actions.	Overload.
Stability of rules and procedures through pre-loading.	Not letting go of expectation of normality.
Transparency of decision-making in times of normality.	Preoccupation with abnormality.
Empowerment and development of capabilities beyond normal operations.	
Provision of tools and techniques that deal with the unexpected (e.g. scenario planning, simulations).	
Idle capabilities during normal times.	

Key decision makers in this scenario are generally compliant with rules and procedures, and in this sense 'normal' operations can tend to look like mode 2, above. Nevertheless, they are also explicitly empowered, authorised and skilled to deal with situations that go beyond normality. Once an unexpected event strikes, they are prepared to deal with this situation (see Table 8.3) and can 'switch' to a more mindful approach.

Although preparedness for dealing with uncertainty can be activated at any time, there are issues with this approach. The first one is overload. The project leader may have his or her hands full dealing with the day-to-day activities of the project. He or she may therefore not have the extra capacity to be mindful and thus to be able to act in this way when required. In addition, the leader's readiness to enact these capabilities may be challenged by a reluctance to 'let go' of normality. This is a shift in emphasis that can be difficult. Similarly, we have also observed a preoccupation with the new abnormality and, as a consequence, the project leader may focus on the urgent situation and largely ignore the rest of the project that still needs attention.

Mindful capabilities are often available pre-crisis and yet are exercised only minimally since the rule-based approach is dominant. Flexible responses under conditions of certainty are neither particularly warranted, nor valuable and the 'idleness' of this capability can be an issue. The mindfulness response repertoire may begin to atrophy if not used, limiting the leader's ability to call upon it in times of need. There is also a corresponding challenge with timely activation, as the leader may be reluctant to allow his or her additional mindful capacities to flourish. As we discussed previously, the project leader may have inherent optimism that the current rule-based path is suitable for dealing with an event and, given his or her emotional attachment to the work, defer the deployment of mindful responses until it is perhaps too late. There is nothing malicious behind this, it is a simple acknowledgement of human nature that we tend to think that we are in control and can do it ourselves.

Pure Mindfulness-based

The final mode by which organisations can deal with uncertainty is one of creating and maintaining permanent mindful capabilities (see Figure 8.6). In this context, there is no (or very limited) preloading of rules and procedures. Decision makers are 'free' to develop their own way of working in contextually separated operations and projects.

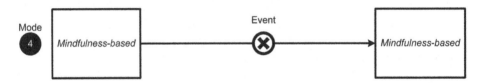

Figure 8.6   Pure mindfulness mode of management

This mode is one of projects being on 'high alert', providing an extensive – and sometimes idle – response repository for engaging with uncertainty (see Table 8.4). We have seen this used successfully in R&D organisations and new product development groups where the environment is necessarily quite uncertain and planning a project in detail at the outset is unlikely to reflect how the future will actually unfold. The problem of such an approach lies in establishing and maintaining such a flexible culture of alertness, reporting and readiness to act on the unexpected. It is difficult to build a mindful organisational culture, yet relatively easy to undermine it by punishing unexpected failure, 'shooting the messenger' or sending the message that staff have transgressed protocols.

Table 8.4   Insights into preparedness and readiness of pure mindfulness mode of management

Preparedness	Readiness
Time and resource intensive.	Continuous alertness to act on abnormalities.
Freedom to develop context-specific ways of working.	Reduced delay in reacting to critical incidents.
Effectiveness (e.g. in innovation) over efficiency (e.g. consistency of action).	Alertness may be compromised by the absence of incidents of abnormality.
Overload of responsibility.	

Most of what we have described is likely to increase the capability to be mindful. Although this is dependent on flexible, situated, human cognition, some of its aspects can be turned into organisational routines. These can then be applied consistently and repeatedly, without appearing unusual or out of place. For example, scenario planning lends itself to regular implementation and can be used to increase accuracy about risk. However, it is important to recognise that its use depends on careful thinking and sensible application to explore possible options – a 'mindless', 'autopilot' approach has only limited value.

The potential difficulty with a fully mindful approach is that its value can erode over time if participants begin to believe that past actions will cover future problems. The purpose of mindfulness, with all its ramifications, is to produce a state of constant challenge and questioning. This tends to be uncomfortable. It is important to be aware of the point at which we begin to believe that we have been successful in dealing with risk – at this point managers need to reinforce the view that there will always be uncertainty out there that makes past action redundant.

WHAT THE LITERATURE SAYS ABOUT ...

Further Reading

We are not the first to write about organisational resilience or rule-based versus mindfulness-based approaches in organisations and projects. For further reading, there is a range of books that we deemed central in writing this synthesis:

- Weick, K. and K. Sutcliffe, *Managing the Unexpected: Assuring High Performance in an Age Of Complexity* [2]: This book builds on the pioneering work of a concept called High Reliability Organisations.

Unlike many other books written by academics, it is easily accessible to practitioners. It offers a compelling insight into a variety of disasters, and provides practical advice on how to establish and maintain a state of collective mindfulness, for the purpose of reliable and resilient performance.

- Hopkins, A. (ed.), *Learning from High Reliability Organisations* [3]: This is a succinct piece of work that looks exclusively at the airline industry. It goes into detail about what makes that industry so reliable, despite the challenges of risk, uncertainty and complexity. It is very much written from a resilience engineering perspective, with a focus on the hard factors of rules, procedures and tools.
- Snook, S.A., *Friendly Fire: The Accidental Shootdown of US Black Hawks over Northern Iraq* [4]: Snook delves into a 'blue-on-blue' incident in the No-Fly Zone over Iraq in 1994, with the loss of 26 military personnel. He provides a fascinating account of the events leading to that fateful shooting down, from multiple perspectives. He avoids the definition of a root cause but acknowledges that a multitude of behavioural factors in combination led to this disaster. His analysis is so contextual that it makes generalisation beyond that incident difficult, but it makes one appreciate the complexity and thus the difficulty of preventing such an incident from happening again.
- Perrow, C., *Normal Accidents* [5]: This book could be interpreted as saying that accidents are bound to happen due to the complexity and uncertainty inherent in an environment. They are hence 'normal'. Perrow offers insights into a variety of disasters, including the role of people as a contributing factor. He categorises industries according to 'coupling' and 'interactions', and so offers an interesting take on how vulnerable each industry is to a 'normal accident'. One may argue that, in Perrow's view, the glass is half-empty, whereas with Weick it is half-full. It is a great counterargument to Weick and Sutcliffe's book on High Reliability Organisations, although with similarities in content.
- Reason, J., *The Human Contribution: Unsafe Acts, Accidents and Heroic Recoveries* [6]: This is probably the most updated account of human situated cognition. Reason captures the audience through his style of writing as well as his in-depth insight into the abyss of the human mind, but tells us that there is help.
- Langer, E.J., *Mindfulness* [7]: One might, just might, consider this book as the foundation for many of those previously-mentioned on mindfulness, a key angle in this book. Yet, Langer is not explicitly mentioned or acknowledged in any of those. She wrote this book on individual mindfulness, whereas Weick, Hopkins and others elevated mindfulness to a collective level. If you would like to explore your own individual resilience, this book is a good start. Langer offers four key dimensions of mindfulness:

Novelty Seeking. Propensity to explore and engage with novel stimuli. This refers to a tendency to perceive every situation as 'new'. This type of person is likely to be more interested in experiencing a variety of stimuli, rather than mastering a specific situation.

Novelty Producing. Propensity to develop new ideas and ways of looking at things.

Engagement. Propensity to become involved in any given situation. An individual who scores high in engagement is likely to see the 'big picture'.

Flexibility. The flexible individual believes in the fluidity of information and the importance of welcoming a changing environment rather than resisting it. Flexibility in this case refers to someone who can view a situation from multiple perspectives and recognise that each perspective has equal value.

The Best Fit?

We identified four different approaches to dealing with risk and uncertainty. All have their benefits and all come with their own challenges in producing a state of project resilience.

Mode 1: Pure rule-based – requires an adherence to a predetermined rule-based approach and does indeed provide reliable performance, yet only for those problems for which appropriate rules have been designed. However, the limitations of its response repository are likely to become apparent when uncertainty strikes. From our research, though, the practical response time could be compromised by the requirement to escalate decisions, accompanied by sometimes lengthy discussions of accountability.

Modes 2: Just-in-time and 3: Infusion – involve some preparation for dealing with abnormal incidents, either by permanently equipping decision-makers with mindful capabilities or by temporarily deploying additional resources. Just-in time provides (potentially) greater efficiency in dealing with abnormality, yet may be compromised by overlapping and sometimes conflicting competences between the embedded decision-makers and the external 'parachuted-in' mindful colleagues. This response method may be insufficient if the additional resources are delayed, or if there are blurred boundaries between the 'fixed' and 'temporary' staff. The infusion mode may incur greater waste as, in the absence of uncertainty, mindful capabilities

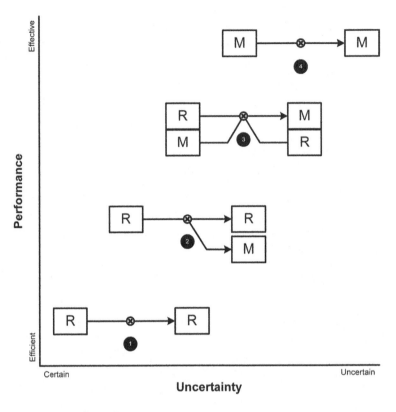

Figure 8.7   The best fit

can remain idle and underutilised. Readiness to enact immediate responses to novel problems can be hampered by the decision-maker's reluctance to acknowledge that abnormality has struck and limited capacity to juggle both normality and abnormality. When activated, the issue of excessive workload might prove detrimental to the management of normal operations.

Mode 4: Pure mindfulness-based – is the one that best accommodates uncertainty and supports innovation but it is the most resource-intensive, requiring a constant state of alertness and flexibility. It may, however, be challenged by complacency over time, and successful utilisation might also lead to calls for greater efficiency. Figure 8.7 indicates the potential suitability of each approach depending on the nature of the environment.

Reflection

In Chapter 1 you assessed your project according to uncertainty/risk. Please think about which mode of resilience your project follows and assess whether there is a mismatch between the environment and your chosen approach.

Which mode of management best describes your project?

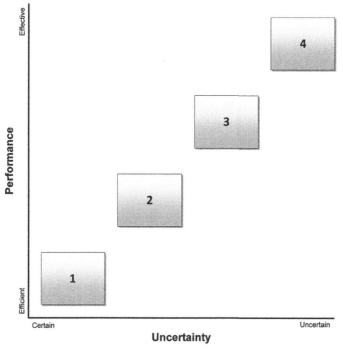

Figure 8.8   Choices for managing adversity

Rocks on the Roads to Resilience

In this book we have suggested how one could – emphasis on could – overcome our innate human characteristics and manage a project in a truly resilient manner. It is important to highlight some problems we are likely to face in trying to be resilient enough to weather any storm that might come along.

First, we are constantly challenged by expectations of certainty and thus control. We vote for people who sell us an illusory world of stability, predictability and well-being. In turn, we expect others to plan and control the future, and project owners and sponsors also expect that of us. To put your hand up and argue that the world out there is largely unknowable is a daunting task. Anyone who has tried to 'sell' a project knows that it is more advantageous to pitch it as (reasonably) certain. Presenting your plan as largely unpredictable, but nonetheless resilient, is a tougher prospect. Even if both the presenter and the audience realise, deep-down, that there are aspects which remain unknowable, it is more comforting to go with a confident, 'traditional' planned approach. Of course, as long as this remains the case, life as a project manager is likely to be challenging.

Such expectations are consistent with what we are longing for as individuals. We seek the comfort of certainty and the sense that we are in control of our lives. By default we do try and build a comfort zone around ourselves. This book suggests that we, maybe tentatively at first, should step across this boundary, moving beyond the tangible and measurable – the risk horizon – and start to be uncomfortable and thus more vigilant, prepared, and ready for uncertainty. For many of us, this might be too uncomfortable even though we may fully recognise the benefits.

Let us now consider resilience along the lines of S.M.A.R.T. goal-setting:

- Specific. Resilience remains largely unspecific, as it relates to human behaviour under a range of different conditions. It cannot be clearly defined or identified according to a given set of practices one has to carry out. In fact, since it is context-specific it thus requires – every time from scratch – a unique match between a problem and a solution. The details of each case will vary. The containment can be prepared and readied for, yet the responses need to be crafted according to unfolding events.
- Measurable. The costs of resilience may be immediately measurable whereas the benefits may be far less tangible. The expected effect of being resilient is based to some extent on faith rather than unarguable financial measurement. The value of resilience could be quantified by the absence of failure. Nevertheless, if such an assessment can only be carried out ex-post, then what benefit does it have?
- Attainable. Unfortunately, there is no agreed state of resilience that is 'good enough' for a project. A state of resilience is an ideal one that that the project team can aspire to, but it is a continual journey rather than a destination. One may consider developing levels of 'resilience maturity', yet it is difficult to take into account the ever-changing nature of risk, uncertainty and complexity.

- **R**elevant. This aspect is in the eye of the beholder and depends on the context. Resilience will probably focus on mindful practices, rather than having choices overly-constrained by the rigid application of rules and procedures. Relevance needs to be considered with regard to the localised assessment of risk, uncertainty and complexity.
- **T**ime-based. Resilience is a permanent state of rule- and mindfulness-based project management. The only time-based dimension refers to when the project context changes and the team needs to adapt to a shifting environment.

Does this imply that resilience is an elusive concept, as it is not S.M.A.R.T.? Yes and No. The 'patchwork' of lures, best practices and suggestions may be turned into a step-by-step guide to follow and apply. S.M.A.R.T. but not 'smart', as the underlying context is central to the choices that need to be made. We would advise against turning the insights of this book into an 'autopilot'. Acknowledge and embrace the lack of specificity, measurability and attainability and use these voids to think about what you can do afresh on your latest project. Try and resist the temptation to think that only what is measurable is automatically good. Resilience is a state, seemingly elusive, often apparently just out of reach. We strive for it, challenge it constantly, yet never manage to reach that ideal state that makes a project truly failsafe. Do you feel uncomfortable enough with this truth?

BEST PRACTICE

Our Case Companies

In order to develop these small vignettes, TTP, Aviva and Intel allowed us to have some insights into their management of projects. In this respect, we are very grateful to have spent time with some of their project managers. Richard Mason and Simon Kelly of Intel talked us through some of the projects they have been involved with. Lynn Newman from Aviva elaborated on best practices, and Tristan Barkley and Piers Harding from TTP provided us with plenty of information about their radical innovation projects.

We asked rather naive questions about how to manage adversity. The purpose was to unravel the obvious. The case companies said that they just do this because they believe it is the right thing to do, although at times they are not aware 'why'. We, the authors, left these vignettes very much unjudged, only summarising what we thought was worth mentioning. If you come to the conclusion that you yourself do what has been mentioned here, please ask yourself, 'why'?

Despite the number of vignettes, neither we nor the respondents can claim that the organisations in which all these projects are embedded are perfect in the sense that no adversity will ever strike. These projects are not 'fail-safe'. Yet, we have chosen these organisations as we believe they each go beyond process, do not put being compliant to rules and procedures centre-stage, and exploit the power of the human mind to deal in particular with uncertainty.

Being resilient through reliance on rule-based and mindfulness-based management is the pursuit of an ideal state, which we can never fully achieve. We can only strive for it. And so do these organisations.

Towards an Art of Resilience

The concept of resilience, in permanent organisations or in temporary projects, is not new to either academics or practitioners. There is, though, a plethora of evidence about the usefulness of reducing human cognition as a source of error by replacing it with rules, applied consistently and transparently. The weight of such evidence seems overwhelming, measured by the number of planning processes and associated accreditation programmes being advocated as 'self-evidently correct'.

Nevertheless, there is growing concern about this single-minded approach to managing risk and uncertainty. This is underlined by major disasters resulting in injury, loss of life and substantial financial costs. A number of alternative approaches are being considered, focusing on the contribution of the mind. However, these progressive discussions on how situated human cognition can benefit the management of uncertainty do not appear to be part of the mainstream of project management, at least from a practitioner's perspective. There is still a very much unchallenged pursuit of ever greater consistency of action. Although our book should be understood as a challenge to conventional wisdom in project management, we cannot claim that it provides the 'Holy Grail' for managing risk, uncertainty and complexity. Evidence about mindfulness and its impact is still limited, although growing, and so this book is more a proposition than a prescription. Its purpose is fulfilled even if you disagree with everything we said. Disagreement is a form of reflection and this book should be a basis for reflection.

You might think after having read all about lures and practices that you already experience all these and that this reflects your reality. It might all be obvious to you and only highlight aspects that you already know. If this is the case, is your project approach as good as it gets? The concept of the resilient project does not claim to offer a universal, complete, set of practices. You probably do much more than has been covered in this book. Bear that in mind, and ask yourself 'why' you do what you do. Does it help you to:

- Notice beyond the risk horizon?
- Interpret uncertainty more realistically?
- Prepare yourself better for the effects of uncertainty?
- Contain uncertainty in a more timely and appropriate manner?
- Recover faster from a crisis?

This book may have helped to start important conversations and may have raised pertinent questions. We hope that our suggestions have been valuable. Our wish is to turn the idea of resilience from an abstract notion to a set of behaviours that make it real for you in your projects and your organisation.

References

1.   Association for Project Management, *Project Management Body of Knowledge*, Anonymous (ed.). 2012, London: Association for Project Management.
2.   Weick, K. and K. Sutcliffe, *Managing the Unexpected: Assuring High Performance in an Age of Complexity*. 2001, San Francisco: Jossey Bass.
3.   Hopkins, A. (ed.), *Learning from High Reliability Organisations*. 2009, CCH Australia: Sydney.
4.   Snook, S.A., *Friendly Fire: The Accidental Shootdown of US Black Hawks over Northern Iraq*. 2000, Oxford: Princeton University Press.
5.   Perrow, C., *Normal Accidents*. 1984, New York: Basic Books.
6.   Reason, J., *The Human Contribution: Unsafe Acts, Accidents and Heroic Recoveries*. 2008, Farnham: Ashgate Publishing.
7.   Langer, E.J., *Mindfulness*. 1989, Camb. MA.: Perseus Publishing.

Index

If you have found this book useful you may be interested in other titles from Gower

**Project Risk Analysis
Techniques for Forecasting Funding Requirements, Costs and Timescales**
Derek Salkeld
9780566091865 (hardback)
9781409444978 (e-book – PDF)
9781409472377 (e-book – ePUB)

Project Ethics
Haukur Ingi Jonasson and Helgi Thor Ingason
9781409410966 (paperback)
9781409410973 (e-book – PDF)
9781409484523 (e-book – ePUB)

**Bridging the Business-Project Divide
Techniques for Reconciling Business-as-Usual and Project Cultures**
John Brinkworth
9781409465171 (hardback)
9781409465188 (e-book – PDF)
9781409465195 (e-book – ePUB)

**Project Management for Supplier Organizations
Harmonising the Project Owner to Supplier Relationship**
Adrian Taggart
9781472411099 (hardback)
9781472411105 (e-book – PDF)
9781472411112 (e-book – ePUB)

GOWER

The Rules of Project Risk Management
Implementation Guidelines for Major Projects
Robert James Chapman
9781472411952 (hardback)
9781472411969 (e-book – PDF)
9781472411976 (e-book – ePUB)

Project Risk Governance
Managing Uncertainty and Creating Organisational Value
Dieter Fink
9781472419040 (hardback)
9781472419057 (e-book – PDF)
9781472419064 (e-book – ePUB)

Exercising Agency
Decision Making and Project Initiation
Mark Mullaly
9781472427885 (hardback)
9781472427892 (e-book – PDF)
9781472427908 (e-book – ePUB)

The Single-Minded Project
Ensuring the Pace of Progress
Martin Price
9781472429964 (hardback)
9781472441447 (e-book – PDF)
9781472441454 (e-book – ePUB)

Visit **www.gowerpublishing.com** and

- search the entire catalogue of Gower books in print
- order titles online at 10% discount
- take advantage of special offers
- sign up for our monthly e-mail update service
- download free sample chapters from all recent titles
- download or order our catalogue